CW00321754

the best ever
ADULT
JOKE
book

the best ever
ADULT JOKE
book

Johnny Sharpe

ARCTURUS

ARCTURUS

This edition published in 2009 by Arcturus Publishing Limited
26/27 Bickels Yard, 151–153 Bermondsey Street,
London SE1 3HA

ISBN: 978-1-84837-175-0
AD001140EN

Printed in the UK

CONTENTS

CONTENTS

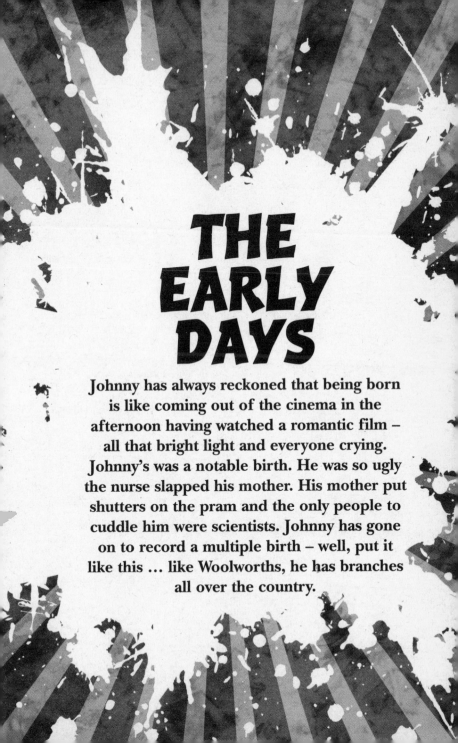

THE EARLY DAYS

Johnny has always reckoned that being born is like coming out of the cinema in the afternoon having watched a romantic film – all that bright light and everyone crying. Johnny's was a notable birth. He was so ugly the nurse slapped his mother. His mother put shutters on the pram and the only people to cuddle him were scientists. Johnny has gone on to record a multiple birth – well, put it like this … like Woolworths, he has branches all over the country.

THE NEW ARRIVAL

The wife's mother rushed into the maternity wing to find out how her daughter was progressing. As she entered the waiting room, she spotted her son-in-law. Unbeknown to her, he was listening to the cricket on his IPod.

"How's it going?" she asked anxiously.

"Not bad," he smiled, "they've got four out and there's only one to go."

"Aaah," she screamed, and fainted.

The 50-year-old woman phoned up her 60-year-old husband.
"Darling, it's a miracle, the doctor says I'm pregnant, isn't that wonderful? You're going to be a father."

"That's great" replied the husband. "By the way, who is this?"

Johnnie asked for time off because his wife was going to have a baby. The following day, his boss asked him what it was – a boy or a girl.

"Too early to say," said Johnny." "it'll be another 9 months before we know the answer to that."

★ ★ ★

"Doctor, doctor, I'm so worried," said the anxious man. "Both my wife and I have black hair, but our son's just been born with red hair. Do you think something funny has been going on?"

"Not necessarily," replied the doctor. "How many times do you have sex?"

"About 5 times a year."

"Well, there's your answer then, you're just a little rusty."

★ ★ ★

MA AND PA

Daddy is mowing the lawn when his young son comes running out of the house calling to him.

"Daddy, daddy, what's sex?" asks the boy.

For a moment dad is dumbstruck but then decides that if his son has asked the question, then he must do his best to answer it. For the next few minutes dad talks about the birds and the bees, then human relationships, love, the sex act, having babies – in fact he does a pretty good job of covering every aspect. Eventually he comes to a stop when he sees how oddly his son is looking at him.

"Why did you want to know?" he asks.

"Well, Mummy said to come out and tell you that dinner would be ready in two secs."

Man to son:
Endeavour to marry a girl with small hands, it'll make your penis look bigger.

"Mummy, mummy, I've discovered how babies are made. I saw daddy put his willy in your mouth last night."

"No, that's not right," replied mummy, "that's how I get my expensive jewellery."

"Mummy, mummy, what's a pussy?" asked the small boy. His mother went to the encyclopaedia and showed him a picture of a cat.
"That's a pussy," she said.
"Mummy, mummy, what's a bitch?" continued the little boy. Again, mother consulted the encyclopaedia and showed her son a picture of a dog.
But the boy wasn't convinced so he went to his father and asked him what a pussy was. Dad went to his magazine, opened it at the centrefold and drew a circle.
"There you are, son," he said, "that's a pussy."
Then the little boy asked him what a bitch was and dad replied sadly, "Everything outside the circle, son."

"Mummy, mummy, what are you doing?" exclaimed the little boy as he walked into the bedroom to find her sitting on daddy.
"Just flattening daddy's tummy," mum replied.
"I wouldn't bother, when you go out tonight the au pair will only blow it up again."

"Hey June, how about a bit of slap and tickle tonight?"
"Sshh John, don't talk like that in front of the children. Let's use code. Whenever you feel like it, just say, "How about turning the washing machine on."
A few evenings later, June turned to her husband and said, "Shall I put the washing machine on tonight?"
"Don't bother, love, you looked a bit tired so I did it by hand."

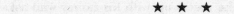

A man gets a peanut stuck firmly in his ear and no matter how hard his wife tries, they cannot get it out. Just as they're about to give up, their daughter arrives home with her boyfriend. When they hear what has happened the boyfriend tells them confidently that he knows how to get it out. He sticks 2 fingers up the man's nose and tells him to blow as hard as he can. The man does this and the peanut pops out. Sometime later the parents are talking and mum comments, "Our Vera's got a clever boyfriend there. I wonder what will become of him."
"I'll tell you one thing, by the smell of his fingers, he'll be our son-in-law," came the reply.

An 18-year-old boy says to his father, "Dad, I keep getting these terrible urges, what can I do about it?"
"I think you'd better go and see my friend Bob, he's a sex

13

therapist, I'm sure he'll be able to help. Pop round to his house this evening."

The boy does as his father suggests, but after 5 visits there's no improvement. The sixth time he goes round the door is opened by Bob's wife who tells him the therapist has been called away on urgent business.

"Can I help at all?" she says.

The boy tells her his problem and within moments she takes him by the hand, leads him upstairs and makes frenzied love to him. The next day he meets up with his father who asks him how the treatment is going.

"It's great now, dad," smiles the boy. "The therapist's wife has got more brains between her legs than he has in his head."

The little girl's mother was entertaining her next door neighbour when her little daughter walked in.

"Hello, Mrs Crabbit, are you a gardening expert?" she asked.

"No I'm not, why do you ask?" said the puzzled neighbour.

"Mum says if there's any dirt about you'll dig it up."

It was cold and pouring with rain but the boy's mother insisted he go and feed the animals on their freeholding before he could have breakfast. The boy went out in a dark rage, kicked the chickens, punched the cow and threw water

14

all over the pigs.

When he got back inside his mother was furious.

"How dare you!" she fumed.

"For that you get no eggs because you kicked the chickens, no milk because you thumped the cow and no bacon because of the way you treated the pigs."

Just then, dad came down the stairs and nearly tripping over the cat, he gave the animal a mighty kick. The boy turned to his mother and said, "Are you going to tell him or shall I?"

A little girl went into her parents bedroom to find her parents in bed.

"Well!" she exclaimed. "And you tell me off just for sucking my thumb."

A very rich businessman asked his small son what he would like for Christmas.

"A baby brother please," he replied.

"I'm sorry, son, there's not enough time, it's only 3 weeks to Christmas."

"Well, can't you put more men on the job?" the son suggested.

15

The farmer and his wife are entertaining the local bigwigs when their son runs in and announces to his father in a loud voice, "Dad, dad, the bull's fucking the cow."
After a moment of shocked silence, the farmer turns to his son and calmly says, "Next time, son, be a little less explicit. You should have said:
"The bull is surprising the cow. That sort of language comes from associating with riff-raff."
Lo and behold, the following week the farmer and his wife are entertaining again when their son rushes in.
"Dad, dad, the bull is surprising the cows."
"Well done, son, you've remembered what I told you, but you should have said the bull is surprising the cow … it can only surprise one cow at a time, you know."
"But he can, dad," insists the boy "He's fucking the horse."

One evening father passed his daughter's bedroom and heard her saying her prayers. Smiling to himself, he stopped to listen and heard her say, "God bless mummy, God bless daddy, God bless Grandpa, bye bye Grandma."
How odd, thought father, but he didn't want his daughter to know he'd been listening so he didn't say anything to her. But tragically, next day Grandma collapsed and died. A few months went by and one evening father heard his daughter praying again.
"God bless mummy, God bless daddy, bye bye Grandpa. No, it couldn't mean anything thought father apprehensively, but

next morning they received a telegram to say that Grandpa had passed away in his sleep!

The household got back to normal and almost a year passed before father heard his daughter again.

"God bless mummy, bye bye daddy."

Absolutely panic-stricken, father stayed up all night, too frightened to sleep in case he didn't wake up. The next morning he walked to work instead of taking the car, in case there was an accident, and spent the day at his desk doing very little but worrying. When he got home that evening he collapsed into a chair, his nerves in pieces, and told his wife all about the nightmare day that he'd had.

She replied, "You're not the only one to have had a bad day. This morning when I opened the front door I found the gasman dead on the front doorstep."

Daddy was taking his young son for a walk in the park when they passed two dogs humping. When the boy asked his father what was happening he told him they were making a puppy. A few days later the little boy caught his mum and dad in the throes of sex and when he asked them what they were doing, dad replied they were making a baby.

The little boy said, "Well, can you turn mummy over, I'd much rather have a puppy."

EARLY LEARNING

Two kids were arguing in the playground.

"My dad's a better darts player than your dad," said the first boy.

"No he ain't," said the second boy. "My dad got the highest score last week."

"OK, OK, but my mum's better than your mum."

"Yeah, alright, my dad says the same thing."

The boy's father was so disappointed with his son's school report, he decided to go and see the headmaster to find out what had gone wrong.

"Well, I have good news and bad news," replied the headmaster.

"The bad news is that your son has discovered he's gay and he spends all his time pursuing the good looking boys instead of studying."

The father was horrified.

"But what on earth is the good news?" he stammered.

The headmaster smiled. "Well, the good news is that your son has been voted Queen of the May."

Father walks into his son's bedroom to find him lying face down on a life-size picture of Britney Spears.

"Son, what's going on?" gasps his father.

"It's alright, dad, I've got plain Jane from next door underneath."

At the end of the human biology class, the lecturer conducted a quick question and answer session to check that everyone had been listening to his lesson.

"You over there, the girl in red," he said pointing, "which part of the body becomes 10 times its normal size under emotional stress?"

Flushed with embarrassment, the girl refused to answer, so another student volunteered.

"The pupil of the eye, Sir."

"Correct," replied the lecturer and he turned to the girl, saying, "Young lady, your refusal to answer my question indicates three things. One, you haven't been listening to my lecture, two, you are obsessed with sex, and three, you are going to be very disappointed."

Class 3 have a boy who is always in trouble, he is constantly upsetting the other children and damaging the school property. Eventually, a letter is sent home to his parents saying the school has put up with his bad behaviour long enough. This morning, they found him masturbating in class so they have expelled him. The letter continues: "I suggest you talk to your son about his dirty little habit as soon as possible. Tell him he'll go blind if he carries on. Yours sincerely, Headmaster."

When the boy's dad hears about the expulsion, mum suggests he goes upstairs and has a "heart-to-heart" with his son and also explain what might happen if he continues masturbating. So dad goes upstairs, into his son's bedroom and starts to talk to him.

"Wait a minute, dad," says the boy, "I'm over here."

A young boy walked into a bar and asked for a bottle of beer and 20 fags.

"Now, now," smiled the barmaid, wagging her finger. "Do you want to get me into trouble?"

He replied, "Not at the moment, I just want my beer and fags."

"Mummy, mummy, are little birds made of metal?"

"Of course not, darling, why do you think that?"

"I just heard dad say he'd like to screw the arse off the bird next door."

Grandpa and Grandson go out together for a day's fishing. At lunchtime, the man opens a can of cider.

"Can I have some, Grandpa?" asks the boy.

"I tell you what, son," replies Grandpa. "Can your willy touch your backside?"

"No, Grandpa."

"Then you can't have any cider."

Later on, Grandpa gets out his cigarettes.

"Can I have one, Grandpa?"

Grandpa replies, "Can your willy touch your backside?"

"No."

"Then it's no to a cigarette."

On the way home, they pass a newsagent's and each of them buys a scratch card. Grandpa wins nothing, Grandson wins £2,000.

"Are you going to share some of your winnings with me, son?" asks Grandpa.

The boy replies, "I tell you what, can your willy touch your backside?"

"It sure can," replies Grandpa confidently.

"Then go fuck yourself."

A group of young boys were always getting into trouble on the estate so the local vicar decided to intervene and speak to each of them about their behaviour. When it was Johnny's turn to go in, he sat down nervously wondering what was going to happen. As with the other boys, the vicar

21

decided to find out how much the boy knew about God and whether he understood the difference between right and wrong. The vicar began with the question, "Where is God?"

Johnny stared at him in amazement but did not answer. Again the question was asked, this time more forcibly.

"I said, where is God," he bellowed.

Frightened out of his skin, Johnny raced from the room, ran all the way home and hid in the wardrobe. His older brother followed him upstairs and shouted through the door.

"What's happened?"

"Oh Tom, we really are in trouble this time. God has gone missing and they think we did it."

Two young hedgehogs were learning survival tactics from their father.

"Today, I want to tell you about one of our biggest dangers. That road out there," instructed dad. "There will be times that you need to cross it and if you're lucky, a car won't come along. But if it does, just make sure that you stop in the middle of the road so it will go over you without touching. Just watch me and you'll see what I mean."

Dad went out into the middle of the road and waited patiently for a car.

"It's coming," he shouted, "now you'll see what…" He never finished speaking. The two young sons heard a sickly crunch as he was flattened on the road.

"I meant to ask him what we should do if a 3-wheeler came along," said one to the other.

The number of children attending Sunday School had dropped dramatically and it was thought that perhaps the lessons had become too serious. As it so happened, a visiting Minister had come to stay and the vicar asked him if he would mind speaking to the children a bit more informally. "Of course," replied the Minister and he sat with the children in a circle saying "First of all, children, can you tell me what eats grass, goes moo, and gives us milk?"
For a moment, there was complete silence and then one small boy slowly put his hand up.
"Please Sir, I suppose the answer is Jesus but it sounds just like a cow to me."

A simple young man is encouraged to broaden his knowledge by learning how to parachute. After a few lessons it's time for his first jump, so that afternoon he and his instructor go up in a plane. The instructor tells the man not to worry because he'll jump straight after him.
So the man jumps out, pulls his rip cord and heads gently for earth. A moment later the instructor jumps out but when he pulls his rip cord nothing happens and within seconds he passes his pupil and plummets to earth at an amazing speed.

"Oh no you don't," says the young man on seeing his instructor race pass.

"You didn't tell me it was a race." At that, he undoes his parachute and shouts gleefully, "Last one home is a sissy."

There was a skinny young boy who was constantly being teased by the older lads in the village. One of their favourite games was to prove how stupid he was by giving him the choice of picking a 20p piece or a 10p piece. The boy always chose the 10p piece which would send the bullies into fits of laughter.

"See," they would say. "He always picks the 10p because it's bigger. He's so thick."

On a number of occasions this trick had been witnessed by the local storekeeper who eventually took the lad aside and questioned him. "I'm sure you know 10p isn't worth as much as 20p, is it really because it's bigger?"

"Of course not," whispered the boy, "but if I stopped picking the 10p they'd stop playing the trick!"

Two six-year-old boys are standing in the toilet having a pee. One turns to the other and says, "Your dinky doesn't have any skin on it."

"That's because I've been circumcised," he replies.

"Cor! What does that mean?"

"It means the skin's been cut off the end."
"How old were you when they did that?"
"About two days old."
"Did it hurt?"
"It sure did. I didn't walk for a year."

Now young Tom, born and brought up in the city, was given a chance to visit his cousin who lived on a farm in the country. It was all very strange to him, particularly when he went into the milking shed and saw all the cows attached to the milking machines and the milk pouring out into the buckets. As soon as he was left alone, he decided to attach the machine to his dick to see how it felt.

Some time later, his cousin returned to find Tom writhing on the floor in great distress.

"What the hell's going on?" exclaimed his cousin.

"Help me, please help me. I stuck my dick in your milking machine and I can't get it out. This is the eighteenth time I've come!"

"Well now, Tom," said his cousin, "I don't think I can turn the machine off either, but don't fret. We'll feed you and look after you. The good news is that it's only set for a gallon and then it'll automatically switch off."

LEAVING SCHOOL

When it came to jobs, the Sharpes' had a great tradition in the iron and steel industry. Johnny's mother used to iron while his father used to steal. Eventually, the time came for Johnny to leave school and he took up his first job as a carpet fitter. Alas, he was soon on the dole after asking his first female customer if she would enjoy a good springy shag and would she like felt underneath? Fortunately the employment sun shone again and Johnny became a specialist in the baking industry in the West Country – he got the job of putting the hairs on the Cornish pasties.

CLUBBING

A naive young man was encouraged to dance with one of the village girls. As the dance became faster, one of the girl's earrings dropped off and fell down her back.

"Be a darling and get that for me," she asked her partner.

"Yes," he stammered, but the more he reached for it, the further down her back it fell.

"Ahem," he said, blushing madly. "I feel a perfect arse."

"Really? Thank you, my tits are pretty good as well."

There's a badminton competition at the local leisure centre and a young man, seeing a girl all on her own, decides to go and ask her if she would like to team up with him for a doubles match. Much to his astonishment she yells at the top of her voice, "How dare you. No I will not join you for a quickie in the back of your car!"

The room falls silent and all eyes are turned to the young man who shuffles away totally embarrassed and humiliated. Ten minutes later the girl approaches him full of apologies and explains that she is experimenting with people's reactions to different situations as part of her thesis on human behaviour. As she finishes talking he exclaims very loudly, "£200! You've got to be joking, I can get it much cheaper elsewhere."

Tom was so shy he'd never had the courage to ask a girl out so his mate Jack decided to take him out on the town and get him laid. Halfway through the evening they were drinking in a nightclub when a girl at the other end of the bar winked at Tom.

"Hey, Jack," he stuttered, "that girl over there winked at me. What shall I do?"

"Wink back," said Jack.

A little later she smiled at him.

"Hey, Jack, she's smiling at me now."

"Well, smile back," said Jack.

A moment later he turned to his mate again and gasped, "Jack, Jack, she's just leant forward and shown me her tits. What should I do?"

"Show her your nuts," said Jack who was busy chatting up someone else.

So Tom turned to face the girl, put one finger in his ear, one finger up his nose and hollered like a jackass.

Dancing together for the first time, the man turned to his partner and said, "My dear, do you know the minuet?"
"Good gracious, no, I don't even know all the men I've laid."

Three men went out on the town and landed up at a sleazy nightclub. As they drank their beers, a naked go-go dancer performed on the table in front of them and at the end of the dance the audience showed its appreciation by throwing her money. The first man grinned at his mates, took £10 out of his pocket and stuck it on the girl's backside. The second man got out a £20 note and stuck it on her fanny. Now the third man had almost spent up but he didn't want to be financially embarrassed in front of the other two. Suddenly, he had a great idea, he took out his credit card, swiped it down her crack and took the £30.

THE MOVIES

Taking his girlfriend to the cinema, the man's wig fell off when they were canoodling in the back row. As he felt around trying to find it, his hand accidentally went up his girlfriend's skirt.

"Oooh…" she moaned, "Go on, go on, that's it."

"No, it can't be," he said. "I part mine on the right."

Little Red Riding Hood was walking through the woods when she was suddenly attacked by a huge wolf.

"At last, at last," laughed the wolf. "I'm going to eat you all up."

"Oh sod it," said Little Red Riding Hood, "doesn't anyone fuck these days?"

While on holiday, the Seven Dwarfs visit the local convent to buy some souvenirs. They meet up with the Mother Superior and Dopey stops to talk to her.

"Excuse me, your holy one, do you have any short nuns here?" Mother Superior is quite puzzled by the question but replies, "Not very short, some around 5 foot."

"Are you sure there aren't any nuns about 3 foot in height?" he persists.

"No, no, no one like that."

As the dwarfs leave, the Mother Superior follows them quietly down the road to try and discover the reason for such an odd question. She overhears the other dwarfs asking him what was said, and he replies, "She said they don't have any." On hearing this, the dwarfs fall about laughing and chanting: "Dopey's fucked a penguin, Dopey's fucked a penguin."

How did Pinocchio find out he was made of wood?
His hand caught fire.

Sherlock Holmes and Doctor Watson went on a camping trip to Dartmoor and as they lay down for the night Sherlock Holmes said, "Doctor Watson, my old friend, when you look up into the darkness, please tell me what you see."

"Well, I can see a very clear sky, there are no clouds and the stars are out in their millions. I can see the Milky Way and I believe that extra bright star over there is the planet Venus which you can see at this time of the year. I would also deduce that being such a clear night will mean that it will get quite chilly."

Watson laughed and said, "But knowing you, Sherlock, I'm

sure there are many things I have missed. What have you deduced?" There was a moment's silence and then Holmes replied, "Somebody's nicked our tent."

The Lone Ranger and Tonto have just spent a month riding through the desert before landing up at Prickly Gulch Creek where they go into the saloon for a much needed drink. They've only been in there a few minutes when a man runs in asking if anyone owns a big white horse.

"That's mine," replies the Lone Ranger. "Is there anything wrong?"

"Sure is, the animal's collapsed," says the man.

The Lone Ranger and Tonto go outside to see poor Silver lying prostrate on the ground, but after giving him some water he seems to revive a bit. The Lone Ranger turns to Tonto and says, "Will you just run around him for a few minutes so he can feel a breeze and that'll soon put him right."

Tonto starts to run around Silver while the Lone Ranger goes back inside to finish his drink. A moment later another man rushes in asking who owns the white horse outside.

"Bloody hell," says the Lone Ranger. "That's mine, now what's wrong?"

"Oh your horse is alright," says the man, "but you've left your injun running."

Two women are watching a film in the cinema when one turns to the other in surprise.

"You're not going to believe this, Mav, but the man sitting next to me is masturbating."

"Dirty bugger, just ignore him," she hisses.

"I can't, he's using my hand."

A cowboy walks into a saloon wearing a paper suit and is immediately arrested by the sheriff for rustling.

A man walks into a saloon, draws his gun and shoots the piano player dead.

"I've been itching to do that for a long time," he says, "that bloody noise has been driving me mad."

The barman beckons the man to one side.

"Mind if I give you a bit of advice, Mister? If I were you I would file off any sharp edges on your gun and grease the barrel."

"Is that supposed to make me a better shot?" asks the cowboy.

"No, but you'll find it'll make things easier for you. That piano player you just killed has two big, mean brothers and when news gets to them about what you did, they'll shove that gun right up your arse."

Peter was hooked on gambling and more than half his wages each week would be lost on this addiction – from the horses, dogs and more obscure pastimes such as cock fighting and ferrets. One evening, he was returning home after becoming champion for keeping a ferret down your trousers for the longest time, when he passed the local cinema and discovered they were showing a film he badly wanted to see. No animals were allowed inside but that was no problem. Peter stuck the ferret down his trousers. Halfway through the picture, he unzipped his flies to give the animal some air. A young girl was sitting next to him and she suddenly nudged her friend and whispered frantically, "Sharon, that man's got his dick out!"

"Sshh, just ignore him," replied her friend.

"But I can't," she moaned, "it's nibbling my knee."

A very popular film was being shown at the local cinema and the place was packed. Suddenly a woman stood up and with a scream rushed out into the foyer to search out the manager.

"I'll never come back here again," she complained. "I've just been interfered with."

A short while later another woman ran out looking distressed, complaining of the same thing.

"I'm not having this," said the manager and he decided to

track down the pervert. Shining his torch along the rows he eventually discovered a man crawling along under the seats. "What the hell do you think you're doing?" he roared.
"It's my toupee," replied the man. "I've lost it. I had my hand on it twice, but it got away."

Deep in the heart of Sherwood Forest, Robin Hood was lying in bed in his cottage, only a few days from death.
"Little John," he croaked "give me my bow and arrow and open the window. I will fire the arrow and wherever it lands, please bury me there."
And indeed, a few days later, Robin died and having promised to carry out his final wish, Little John and the rest of the Merry Men buried Robin on top of the wardrobe.

THE LAW

The woman was up in court for a second time, filing for divorce. Three years earlier she had divorced her first husband because she claimed his "tackle" was too big. This time she wanted a divorce because her husband was "too small."

The judge granted her divorce but just before she left the court he gave her some words of warning.

"Madam, this court does not want to see you here again so be careful how you choose a third husband. We have more important things to do than sort out the right fitting for you."

★ ★ ★

One day while on traffic control, a policeman flags down a car for speeding. As he walks up to the car he sees it is being driven by a beautiful brunette.

"Excuse me, Miss, did you not see the signs, this is a 30 mph zone and you were going at least 50 mph. May I see your licence and insurance please?"

"Oh dear," replies the dizzy girl. Do you mean these, officer?" and she hands him some documents from her bag.

"That's right, Miss, won't be a moment", and with that he walks over to his car to radio in the details.

"I think I know this woman," comes the reply, "is she a dizzy brunette?"

"Yes, why?"

"Just go back over and take your trousers down."

"What the fuck are you talking about?" says the policeman in amazement.

"Don't worry, just do as I say, it'll be fine."

So the policeman returns to the woman's car, hands back her documents and drops his trousers.

"Oh wow," she replies, "not another breathalyser."

It was late at night and the police were out checking for erratic driving. They spotted a car travelling alone along the dual carriageway and decided to follow it. The car never exceeded the speed limit, gave all the correct signals as it left the main road and when they reached the town it pulled up correctly at all the traffic lights. Eventually, the police car overtook the car and flagged it down.

"Good evening, Sir," said the policeman.

"We felt we had to stop you to congratulate you on your perfect driving skills."

"Well, thank you, officer," replied the driver, "I always drive very carefully, especially when I've had a bit to drink."

Three country lads were out in the big city when they were attacked by a mugger.

"Give me all your valuables," he hissed, "if you don't

I'll inject you with AIDS."

Immediately, two of the lads handed over their wallets and then ran away. The third lad, however, refused so the mugger injected him. Later, when the three lads met up, the two who had handed over all their money looked at their friend aghast.

"Don't you realise what he's done? You've been injected with AIDS."

The third lad smiled.

"No, no, it's alright, I'm wearing a condom."

"You are up before this court for the hideous crime of making love to your wife after she had died. Do you have anything to say in your defence?"

"Yes, your honour. I didn't know she was dead, she'd been like that for years."

A music hall entertainer is stopped by the police for having a faulty break light, and on the back seat of the car, the policeman spots a whole set of knives. He asks the man why he has them – doesn't he know it's against the law to carry knives.

The man explains that the knives are used in his act – he juggles them.

The policeman insists the man gets out to show him so he

stands at the roadside performing his act. Just then, another car drives by and the driver turns to his wife, saying, "Thank goodness I gave up the demon drink, just look how the police test you these days."

A man stumbles into the police station yelling blue murder that his car has been stolen.

"Can you tell me where you left it, Sir?" asks the duty sergeant.

"On the end of this bloody key," he screeches.

Now it had been a difficult evening and the duty sergeant's temper was at boiling point. He retorted, "Listen here, you wretched little man, you're so bloody drunk, you can't remember anything and your whole behaviour is disgraceful. Why! you've even left your flies undone."

"Fucking hell," slurred the drunk, "they've stolen my girlfriend as well."

The traffic police flag down a car for driving erratically and ask the driver, a young girl, to step out of the car and take a breathalyser test. As they look at the results, the policeman turns to the girl and remarks severely, "You've had a few stiff ones tonight, Miss."

"Oh my goodness," she exclaims blushing. "I didn't know it told you that as well."

"You are up before this court for entering a dog in the local pet show," said the judge. "You will go to prison for 3 months."

"Okay, this is a robbery, everyone down on the floor immediately," shouted the armed raiders as they ran into the bank. Everyone lay face down on the floor except for one girl who lay on her back.
"Hey," whispered her friend, "this is a bank robbery, not the office party, so turn over."

A very drunk man was walking down the street, one foot on the pavement and the other on the road.
"I shall have to arrest you for being drunk," said the policeman.
"Drunk?" said the man. "How can you tell?"
"You are walking with one foot on the pavement and the other on the road," replied the officer.
"Oh that's wonderful" said the drunk, "for a while I thought I had one leg shorter than the other."

42

The traffic police spotted a man staggering towards his car and opening the driver's door. They stopped and confronted him.

"Excuse me, sir, but I hope you are not intending to drive the car?"

"Of course I am, officer," he slurred. "I'm in no state to walk."

A naive young man found himself in the wrong part of town late at night, and got attacked by a gang of muggers. He put up a terrific fight but was eventually overcome and lay bleeding on the ground. When the muggers went through his pockets, all they found was a handful of loose change.

"You went through all that just to protect a few coins?" they asked amazed.

"Oh I see," said the man. "For a while I thought you were after the £500 hidden in my shoe."

"What's wrong, miss?" asked the kindly policeman when he saw the girl crying.

"A thief has just stolen £20 I had hidden inside my knickers," she sobbed.

"Did you try to stop him?"

"I didn't know he was only after my money."

The traffic police flagged down the car.

"Excuse me, Sir, you've just hit four parked cars and driven straight over the middle of the roundabout. It's obvious you are very drunk."

"Officer, thank you so much for telling me. I thought the steering had gone on the car."

The judge turned to the woman and asked, "I see you're divorcing your husband on the grounds that he is a slob and uncouth. Can you give me any examples of this?"

"Yes, your honour. Whenever we go out he always drinks tea with his pinkie sticking out."

"But there's nothing wrong with that," said the judge. "It's considered good manners in some circles to drink tea with the little finger sticking out."

"But I wasn't talking about fingers," she replied accusingly.

A gang of notorious bank robbers stormed through the doors waving their guns and demanding all the customers line up against the wall. While some of his men started putting the money from the safe into bags, the leader shouted to his hostages, "Before we go, we're going to rape all the men and rob all the women."

Hearing this, one of the gang turned to him and said, "Boss, you mean rape all the women and rob all the men."
Suddenly a young gay man said, "Hey, he's the boss, you should do as he says."

The judge turned to the farmer and said, "Mr Brown, you are in this court to claim damages against this truck driver, for the awful injuries you sustained at the time of the accident. And yet, Mr Brown, at the time of the accident you were heard to say to the policeman that you'd never felt better. Kindly explain."
"It's like this, your honour" replied the farmer. "At the time of the accident the policeman went over to my dog, and seeing it was so badly injured, he shot it. Then he went over to my two cows and when he saw they had broken legs, he shot them as well. So when he came and asked me how I felt, I thought it was a good idea to tell him I'd never felt better."

Instead of sending two convicted drug dealers to jail, the judge decides to give them both 250 hours of community service.
"You will work in a drug rehabilitation centre, explaining to those poor addicts the evils of drug abuse. After your sentence you will return to me with a full report of your work."

45

The two drug dealers carry out the judge's wishes and return to him at the end of their sentence.

"How did it go?" the judge asks the first man.

"I managed to get 31 people off drugs," he replies.

"Well done, and how did you manage that?"

"I drew two circles – one large and one small. I told them the large circle was the size of their brain before drugs, and the small circle was what their brain would be like after drugs." The judge then asks the second man how he did.

"I got 200 people off drugs," he replies.

"But that's staggering," says the judge. "How did you manage that?"

"Well, I drew two pictures – a small circle and a large circle. I showed them the small circle first and told them that was their arsehole before going into prison …"

A young woman is alone in a railway carriage when a dishevelled lout walks in, sits opposite her and takes out a packet of peeled prawns to eat. Belching and farting, he eats his way through the packet and then throws the empty carton onto the floor.

At this point the young woman gets up, gathers together all the rubbish and throws it out of the window. She then pulls the communication cord.

"You silly bitch," he chuckles, "that'll cost you a £50 fine."

"Maybe," replies the lady. "But it'll cost you 15 years when they smell your fingers."

A simple young man got very drunk one day and was caught short on the way home so he relieved himself in the local river. At that moment a policeman came along and shouted to him.

"Stop that immediately, put it away and go home, you drunken sod."

The man stuck his dick back inside his trousers and started to laugh.

"What the hell are you laughing at?" demanded the policeman.

"Ha, ha," replied the man. "I really tricked you this time. I put it away but I didn't stop."

"Have you anything to say before I pass sentence?" asked the judge.

"Fuck all," said the defendant.

"I'm sorry, I didn't hear that," replied the judge and turning to the clerk of the court, he asked him what the man had said.

"He said Fuck all," responded the court official.

"Really?" puzzled the judge. "I could have sworn I saw his lips move."

47

A simple man was accused of stalking a beautiful young girl and was told he would have to line up in an identity parade. When they took the girl along the line, he shouted loudly, "That's her."

"Mr Makepiece, you are up before this court for possessing a counterfeit press. Although no money can be found, I pronounce you guilty of intent to produce counterfeit money. Do you have anything to say?" asked the judge.
"Just one thing, your honour. You'd better find me guilty of adultery as well because I have the equipment for that too."

"Mr Luckless, before I pass sentence, do you have anyone who could vouch for your good character?" asked the judge.
"Yes, Your Honour, I do," he replied.
"Him over there" and he pointed to the local police officer.
"But your Honour," spluttered the officer, "I've never met this man in my life."
"Exactly," exclaimed Mr Luckless, triumphantly. "I've lived in this town for twenty years and the police still don't know me. Now doesn't that show good character?"

The head of the East End gang was Walter "Shooter" Menagle. He and his thugs earned thousands of pounds a month from protection rackets, gambling syndicates and general crime. One day, one of his trusted men asked him if he could find a job for his nephew who was deaf and dumb. "Sure," said Menagle, "get him to be a runner for the casinos. So young Ken joined the gang and went about his business unnoticed by those around him until one fatal morning when he and his uncle were called to Menagle's office.

"Now listen and listen good," said Menagle to the uncle.

"Your low-down no-good nephew has been stealing money from me. Bit by bit over these past few months, it's added up to over £¼ million. I want it back. NOW. Go on, tell him." The shocked uncle turned to his nephew and in sign language asked him what he had done with the money. Ken shook his head and Menagle flew into a rage. Taking a gun out of his jacket he aimed it at the boy's head and screamed, "Get that fucker to tell me where the money is or he can start to say his prayers."

Again, the uncle asked his nephew in sign language and this time the terrified boy responded by signing that he'd hidden the money in his uncle's garage.

"Well," demanded Menagle. "What's he saying?"

"He said he doesn't believe you'd shoot him, he thinks you'll chicken out."

A fishing boat had crashed onto the rocks in heavy seas and the lighthouse keeper was taken to court for negligence. His lawyer asked him "Did you carry out your duties on the night in question?"

The lighthouse keeper described his work, how the machinery flashed the light on and off and how he constantly watched the seas through his telescope. The jury was so impressed with his testimony that they found him not guilty.

Later, the lawyer congratulated him on being such a clear speaker.

"Thank you," said the lighthouse keeper, "but I was worried for a while."

"How come?" asked the lawyer.

"I was worried that someone was going to ask me if the light was working."

★ ★ ★

The timid man was put in jail for jaywalking and found himself sharing a cell with a huge brute of a man – 19 stone, hairy and rough and doing life for murder.

"Now let's get one thing sorted out straight away," he snarled, "are you going to be the husband or the wife?"

Terrified of the consequences, the poor man stuttered "I, I'll – er – be the husband," thinking it was the better of two evils.

"Okay, husband, grinned the brute. "Get down on your knees and suck your wife's dick."

★ ★ ★

"Mr O'Malley, you are up before this court for being drunk and disorderly. Do you have anything to say in your defence?"

"Yes, your honour. I fell into bad company. I met some non-drinkers in the park."

"But why should that be bad?"

"I had a bottle of whisky with me and I had to drink it all myself."

★ ★ ★

It was a big day in the remote Welsh town because old Lloyd was up in court for indecent behaviour with a sheep. All the townspeople packed into the small court to hear the proceedings. The one and only witness took the stand and was asked what he had seen." Well, your honour, I see's old Lloyd walk up behind this sheep, drop his trousers and hold onto the sheep's back. There was a bit of shaking and then he pulled his trousers back up, and the sheep turned around and licked his face."

At that point, one of the men on the jury turned to his fellow jurors and whispered, "You can tell it's a good sheep when it does that."

"Quite right," said the others, nodding their heads.

★ ★ ★

LOVE'S YOUNG DREAM

The young couple had just got down to business when the girl suddenly stopped.

"What's wrong, sweetheart, am I hurting you, shall I take it out?"

"Yes," she murmured. "Would you mind taking it out and then putting it in a few times until I make up my mind?"

★ ★ ★

"Hello, Colin, what are you doing riding around on that woman's bicycle?"

"Well, it's a long story," replied Des. "I was on my way into town when this lady passes me on a bicycle. She stops, waits for me to catch up, gives me a kiss and then takes her clothes off!"

"You can have anything you want," she says, so I took the bicycle...Well, I'm not a pervert, I don't wear women's clothes."

★ ★ ★

Halfway up a 1 in 4 hill the couple's car spluttered to a halt. "Shall we get out and push it up?" asked the man.

"That's a good idea," she replied, "but will it be alright to leave the car here?"

On another occasion the car broke down on a very cold winter's day.
"I'll soon have it mended," said the man and he jumped out of the car and tinkered about underneath the bonnet. Five minutes later he got back in the car and put his hands between her legs.
"It's so cold out there, my hands are freezing up so I'm just trying to warm them," he explained.
Over an hour went past and every 10 minutes he would jump back in the car to warm up his hands between her legs. On the seventh occasion she turned to him and said, "It's a shame your ears don't suffer from the cold as well."

"Oh my darling," whispered the passionate young man. "Am I the first man you've ever made love to?"
"Yes, yes," she replied, looking bored. "Why do men always ask the same silly question?"

How do you know if your girlfriend's frigid?
When she opens her legs, the light goes on.

A bloke was walking through the park late at night when he stood on a man's bottom.
"Oh thank you," said a girl's voice.

It was 11.30 at night as the young couple made their way back from the pub. Suddenly they could contain their passion no longer and stopping by a fence he took her there and then. Unfortunately their excitement was so boisterous that the fence was knocked down and the sound brought the householder storming down the garden.
"What the hell's going on?" he yelled. "I want £60 now to repair that bloody fence."
The man paid up and later when they were alone, he turned to his girlfriend and said, "Come on, Sylvie, you're always on about equal rights, how about giving me half towards the fence?"
"Get real!" she answered. "You were the one doing all the pushing."

★ ★ ★

What is an outdoor girl?
One with the bloom of youth in her cheeks and the cheek of youth in her bloomers.

The village idiot was getting a lot of teasing from the local boys.

"Hello, Jake," they said. "We hear you've been practising a lot of sexual positions."

"That's right," he said proudly. "I hopes to try them on girls soon."

A rather reticent young girl was asked how she got on with her new boyfriend.

"Let's just say my legs are my best friends," she replied mysteriously.

"Oh come on," said her mate. "What does that mean?"

"It means he came on too strong so I walked home."

A few weeks later the two friends were talking and the girl's mate asked her how her new date went on the previous night.

"Pretty much as before," she replied. "My legs are my best friends."

Time went by and on the third time they met up, the girl looked radiantly happy.

"You're looking well," commented her mate. "Something's doing you good."

"Oh yes," replied the girl. "I've met this wonderful bloke and let's just say even the best of friends must part."

Overheard in a parked car down lover's lane:
"Suck, suck, Emma…blow is just a figure of speech."

Did you hear about the young girl who swallowed a pin when she was 10 and never felt a prick until she was 19?

"Now don't forget," said mother as her daughter went out on her first date, "say no to everything he suggests."
Later on in the evening after they'd been out to dinner he turned to her and asked, "Do you mind if we go back to my place for a bit of sex?"

"Hey darling, what do you think of this photo, it's me posing for the centrefold – good ain't it?" boasted the young man.
"Mmm," replied the girl. "If I were you, I'd get it enlarged."

The boy was so frustrated. He'd been seeing this girl for over a month but apart from some kissing and cuddling, he'd never made a move on her because he was embarrassed

56

at the small size of his willy. Eventually, he plucked up all his
courage took it out and placed it in her hand.

"No thanks," she said, "I don't smoke."

"Why have you got those marks on your knees?" her friend
asked.

"Oh, it's making love, doggie style."

"Well, why don't you change positions?"

"I'm willing, but the dog isn't."

After thrashing away for a good five minutes, the man lay
back on the bed smiling smugly.

"How was it for you, darling, good?"

"Quite painless actually," she replied. "I never felt a thing."

★ ★ ★

Mum walks into the bedroom to find her daughter in fits of
tears.

"Oh mum, it's so unfair. Yesterday, Derek said he'd buy me a
diamond ring if I stayed the night with him. So I did, but all
he bought was a cheap trinket."

"My darling," says Mum. "Always remember this and you
won't fall into the trap again. When they're hard they're soft
and when they're soft, they're hard."

He's called Jack the Whistler because by putting two fingers in his mouth his whistle can be heard over a mile away. One evening, Jack takes his girlfriend down lovers' lane and by the time they're ready to go home it's very late and they catch sight of the last bus disappearing round the corner.

"Quick, Jack, whistle," urges the girlfriend. Jack starts to put his fingers to his mouth but suddenly stops.

"No, I've a better idea," he says. "I feel like a bit of exercise tonight, let's walk."

A young hitch hiker got a lift with a lorry driver but halfway through the night they found themselves stranded on top of the moors. The driver told her they'd have to wait till morning before getting help so she could have his bed in the cabin and he would sleep on the seat. After a while, the girl whispered, "It's a shame you have to give up your bed, why don't you come in with me, there's plenty of room."

So the man got in beside her.

"It might be nice if we slept 'married'," she giggled.

"Whatever you like," he said, and he turned his back to her and went to sleep.

If only the young man had been more sexually experienced! When she asked him if he fancied something from the Karma Sutra, he replied, "Thanks, but not for me. Indian food has me on the toilet all night."

"Hi handsome! Is that a gun in your hand or are you just pleased to see me?"
"It's a gun," he replied.

The man was desperate.
"But Julie, the size of a man's tackle isn't everything. Don't you think a man's personality is more important?"
She replied, "But you haven't much of a personality either!"

"Oh my darling, do you always kiss with your eyes closed?" whispered the smitten young man.
"Only when I have to kiss you," she replied.

"Oh Tracy, I love you," he simpered. "Please tell me there's no one else in your life."
"Of course there's no one else," she replied. "Do you think

I'd go to the cinema with a nerd like you, if there was another man?"

Johnny and Sarah disappeared behind the barn where they were soon rolling around on the ground, shagging for all they were worth. All of a sudden Johnny said, "Heh doll, is my prick in you or in the mud?"
Sarah felt around and replied, "Well I never, it's in the mud."
"Put it back then, sweetheart."
A little later, Johnny asked again, "Is my prick in you or in the mud?"
"Don't worry, it's alright," said Sarah, "it's in me."
"Well, be a sport and put it back in the mud, would you?"

The 20-year-old son of the house was smitten with the au pair who looked after his baby sister. He was sure he was in love and did all he could to attract her attention. Finally, his efforts were successful and he enticed the au pair into bed. But to his horror, he couldn't get Percy to rise and felt profoundly embarrassed.
"Don't worry about it," said the au pair gently. "Sometimes this happens to your father as well."

"Hello, Bert, what a lovely day. Where are you off too?"
"I'm going courting."
"Really! But why are you wearing wellingtons?"
"I've got to have somewhere to put the sheep's back legs."

Steve was a down-to-earth cockney lad from the East End docks of London. At this time, he had a problem and he didn't know what to do. He was in love with two girls and they were in love with him. There was Tracy who worked in her dad's eel pie and mash shop. She was blonde, beautiful and funny. But there was also Maria, dark and stunning, kind and thoughtful. One day he was passing a church and decided to go inside for some divine inspiration. He knelt down in one of the pews and prayed.
"Oh God, please 'elp me. I've gotta decide who to wed, shall I marry Tracy or Maria?"
When he had finished he looked up and smiled gratefully, for over the alter he read "Ave Maria". And that's just what he did.

"What's wrong, Jake, you look all fired up," said his mate.
"I sure am. My girl's going to die of the clap."
"No, don't worry. People don't die of the clap these days."
"They do when they give it to me."

★ ★ ★

An unscrupulous young man had fancied this girl for ages but she had shown no interest in him so he decided to play a trick on her. The next time he saw her sunbathing on the beach he went up and said, "Hi Julie, I bet you £10 I can keep an eye on my clothes while I dive into the sea."

Now Julie felt pretty sure that it would be impossible for him to dive in and watch the beach at the same time so she accepted the bet. The young man took a false eye out of his pocket put it on his clothes and then dived into the water. When he returned he smiled and said, "Come on, Julie, I bet you another £10 I can bite my own ear."

"Oh no," she said, "Not more tricks. I suppose it's plastic teeth this time?"

"I promise you they're my own," he said, so she accepted the bet. He took out his false teeth and bit his own ear. Now Julie was down £20 and feeling very annoyed." Heh Julie, I'll give you a chance to win all your money back. I bet I can make love to you and you won't feel a thing.

"Now Julie knew all about sex and she knew that was impossible so she took the bet. He got down on top of her and away they went. "Ah ah" she said triumphantly. "I can feel you!"

"Oh well," he said grinning. "You win some, you lose some."

62

"Doctor, doctor, my dick has turned yellow, what can I do?" asked the worried young man.

"Well, that's extraordinary," replied the doctor. "Do you work with dyes or chemicals?"

"No, I'm unemployed."

"What do you do all day?"

"I just watch television and eat Quavers."

A nymphomaniac was walking home late at night when she was attacked and raped by a man who had been lying in wait. When it was over he turned to her and said, "What are you going to do now?"

"I'm going to run home and tell my flatmate I've been raped twice ... unless you're not tired yet," she replied.

It was the annual dance at the town hall and a couple were dancing very close together. After a while the girl whispered in his ear, "Why don't we go outside to the car?"

"Oh I don't know," he said. "I like dancing."

But the girl continued to coax him and eventually he agreed. When they got outside it was pitch black so the man produced a torch from his pocket.

"Have you had that torch with you all night?" she asked.

"Yes," he said.

"Oh well, in that case let's go back to the dance."

★ ★ ★

A young girl travelling on a crowded train asked a man if she could have his seat because she was pregnant. The man immediately jumped up and the girl sat down. As the man looked at her he remarked, "You don't look pregnant, how far gone are you?"

"Oh, about 30 minutes," she replied "but it sure is knackering."

★ ★ ★

Three beautiful young girls are walking along the beach when they come across a man sunbathing. He has no arms or legs. The first girl goes up to him and says, "Have you ever been hugged?"

The man shakes his head, so she bends down and gives him a big hug. The second girl asks him if he has ever been kissed. Again he shakes his head so she bends down and gives him a long lingering kiss. Then the third girl asks him if he has ever been fucked.

"No, no," he stammers, his face lighting up in anticipation.

"Well, you are now," she replies "the tide's coming in."

★ ★ ★

Looking through an open bedroom window one night, a Peeping Tom came upon a young couple playing a rather kinky game. Stark naked, they were sitting in opposite corners of the room, a bag of marbles besides the man, and a pile of hoops besides the woman. As he watched the woman threw a hoop and it landed on the man's erect penis. "Hooray!" she said "One to me".

Then the man rolled a marble straight between her legs and cheered "Now it's one all."

The next day the Peeping Tom's wife was going shopping and asked him if there was anything he needed.

"Yes," he replied with a secret grin on his face "A bag of sprouts and a packet of polo mints."

OFF TO WORK

Johnny's time at the pickle factory didn't last long. He'd only been there a week when he came home looking very agitated.

"What's wrong?" asked his friend.

"I've got this terrible urge to put my willy in the pickle slicer."

"Aagh! it'll all end in tears, you've got to overcome this feeling." Johnny promised he'd try but a couple of weeks later he came back looking well pissed off.

"What's wrong, you didn't weaken and put your willy in the pickle slicer."

"I did," replied Johnny, "and you were right, it did end in tears. I got the sack and the pickle slicer – she was fired too."

Johnny goes to work on a farm and is put in charge of the sheep. To his dismay he cannot get them to lamb so seeks advice from an old mate, brought up in country ways.

"Get your sheep in the tractor, take them up to the top of the moors at the dead of night and shag them yourself," says the friend. "Then in the morning if they're lying down they'll be pregnant."

So that night Johnny does as he's been told, takes them up to the moors in his tractor and gives them all a good shagging.

Next morning he looks out of his window but they're all standing up. So next day he tries again, takes them up the moors in his tractor, does the business, but the next morning they're still all standing up. The following night he goes through the routine again but the next morning he's woken up by a terrible noise.

"Bloody hell," he curses, looking down into the farmyard. The sheep are all sat in the tractor sounding the horn.

Johnny tried many different jobs in his younger days. One afternoon he went into the theatrical agent's.

"Yes?" said the agent. "What do you do?"

"Bird impressions," he replied.

"Bloody hell, not another one. Go on, get on with it," said the agent.

So Johnny flapped his wings, shat all over the agent's desk and jumped out of the window.

It was the young girl's first day in her new job as P.A. to the company director. Before she was called in to his room one of the other secretaries took her aside.

"I think I ought to warn you that your new boss is a right old randy devil. He'll rip your dress off at the first opportunity."

"Thanks for warning me," replied the girl. I'll remember to wear an old dress in future."

A young man was told to do the rounds with the old experienced salesman so that he would learn the tricks of the trade. Every time they arrived at a prospective customer, the young man noticed the salesman would always make the sign of the cross before going in – and then more often than not he would make a sale. At last he commented, "I didn't know you had to be a Catholic to do this job."
"I'm not," replied the salesman, "but never see a client before checking your glasses, your wallet, your pen and your flies."

The recruiting officer was giving a lecture on survival to an adult education class at the local college. He laid out all the items from his knapsack including flares, water, chocolate, torch, map, warm clothing etc. plus a pack of cards.
"What are the cards for?" asked one bright spark.
"Ah ha," replied the officer. "Once you've tried all other means of survival, take your pack of cards and lay out a game of patience. You can lay odds that after a couple of minutes some bugger will come along and say black eight on the red nine!"

A flirty young farmer's daughter took her father's prize cows over to the neighbouring farm to be serviced by their bull.

The handsome farmhand brought in the bull and before long there was a flurry of activity.

"Cor, I wish I was doing that," said the farmhand feverishly.

"Well, it's alright by me," replied the girl, smiling coyly.

"Thanks," he said, "but maybe the cow wouldn't like it."

It was like a scene from Baywatch. Three girls were being interviewed for the job of lifeguard and each was asked the question: "What would you do if you saw someone fall off a boat?"

The first said she would race immediately into the water and swim out to rescue them.

The second said she would radio for a medical team to be waiting and then swim out to rescue them.

The third said she would get one of the other lifeguards to go out while she waited on shore for help.

Now which girl got the job?

Why! the one with big tits of course.

It was Open Day on the farm and visitors were being taken round on guided tours. One group was led by a simple minded youth and in the party was a ventriloquist who thought he'd have some fun. Arriving at the horses, the ventriloquist used his voice to make it look as if the horse was saying "Hello there, welcome to our farm."

They moved on to the cows and he made one of the cows look as if it was saying "They've moved us onto the worst field in the farm."

Then the pigs said, "Yes, but it's that dog keeps upsetting the young ones."

By this time the simple farmhand is sweating with anxiety.

"Now look here," he says to the group as they move towards the sheep pen. "Don't believe a word those sheep tell you."

The young man was obsessed by the beautiful secretary in his office. He just had to kiss her and touch her body and …

One day, he plucked up the courage to speak to her.

"I think you're so gorgeous, if I paid you £250, would you come into the storeroom with me so that I can kiss you and rub my hands up and down your body?"

Now the girl liked money a lot, so she agreed and they disappeared into the storeroom. For the next 10 minutes, he showered her with kisses, unbuttoning her blouse and ravishing her breasts, but all the time, he kept murmuring, "I don't know, I don't know."

Eventually, she asked, "Why do you keep saying 'I don't know?"

"Well, I don't know how I'm going to pay you", he replied.

The electrician remarked to his apprentice, "You'll see all sorts of things in this job, lad, but just keep your mind on the work and above all, use tact. Let me give you an example. I was asked to install a new light fitting in number 43 but when I went in, a naked lady was in the shower. I immediately turned round and left, saying, "Excuse me, Sir. Now that is tact!"

A couple of weeks later, the electrician and his apprentice were called to a house on the Vale Estate. They were asked to install new wiring. The electrician asked his apprentice to check out the rooms upstairs but when he came back down, he had two black eyes and a bloody nose.

"What happened to you?" exclaimed the electrician.

"You and your bloody tact," sobbed the boy. "I went into this bedroom and there was a naked couple lying on the bed so I quickly tried to leave, saying "Excuse me, gentlemen" and that's when they hit me!"

After spending six months in a desert outpost, the new recruit goes to see his commanding officer.

"I'm sorry, Sir, but this place is driving me nuts. If only we had some female company."

"Well, I can't do anything about that, son," replies the officer,

"but we do have something else. There's a barrel over there with a hole in the side and you'll find that will help to relieve your frustrations. You're free to use it any day but Wednesday."

"Thank you, Sir," replies the recruit, "but why can't I use it on Wednesday?"
"Well, it's all based on a sharing system and on Wednesdays it's your turn in the barrel."

The simpleton's car broke down and the garage man arrived to take a look at it.
"Oh yeah, shit in the carburettor," said the mechanic.
"Really, how often will I have to do that?" he replied.

"You can use my Dictaphone," said the office Casanova to the new secretary.
"No thanks, I'll use my finger like everyone else," she replied.

The milkman delivers the milk the day before Christmas and rings the bell of number 11, hoping for a festive tip. As the door opens, he sees a beautiful woman standing there wearing a see-through nightie. She takes him by the hand and guides him upstairs where she makes mad passionate love to him. At the end of the session, they return downstairs where she cooks a delicious fried breakfast and hands him £1.

"I don't understand" says the puzzled milkman. "What's going on?"

She replies, "When I asked my husband whether I should give you a £5 tip, he replied, 'Fuck the milkman and give him £1.' The breakfast was my idea."

"Help, help," sobbed the simple lad. "I've cut my finger off in that machine."

"How on earth did you manage that?" said his mate.

"Well, I just put my finger on that spinning wheel...aah... there goes another one."

Camp Ordeal certainly lived up to its name. New recruits to this remote army base dreaded the posting.

One night there was a surprise inspection. The bugle was blown and the young soldiers ran swiftly to quadrangle where they lined up, most of them naked because there wasn't time to put anything on. As the sergeant major walked down the line, he saw that one soldier had a huge erection and quick as a flash he thumped it hard with his baton.

To his amazement, the soldier remained standing perfectly still with a blank look on his face.

"Bloody hell," cursed the sergeant major, "I just swatted your penis and you stand there unaffected."

The soldier replied, "It's not mine sir, it belongs to the man behind."

The young lad was taken on by the local newspaper as a trainee journalist. After a few weeks sweeping up, answering the telephone and generally tidying up, he was sent out on his first assignment. He was off to interview the attendant at the public toilets who had been working there for fifty years.

"I expect you've seen a lot of changes in your time?" asked the boy.

"Oh yes indeed," replied the man, "It's not like it used to be. These days, the kids come in to take drugs – ecstasy, smoke some grass, snort cocaine, even put the needles in themselves." He shook his head sadly and beckoned the boy a bit closer. "To be quite honest with you, now if they come in for a shit, it's a breath of fresh air."

Bob Bright was a trainee manager in the town's largest supermarket. He was doing well, although one day he almost met his match. A customer approached him and asked for half an apple. When he was told this was impossible, the customer insisted and was beginning to make quite a scene. Bob went off to check with his boss.

"Mr Blake, sir, there's some crazy prat out there who wants to buy half an apple."

As he finished speaking, he noticed the customer had followed him in, so he very quickly said, "And this customer would like to buy the other half."

"Then do it," said the boss.

A few weeks went by until one day Bob was called to the boss's office." Aah! there you are, Bob. I was so impressed with the way you handled that awkward situation the other day – such quick thinking – that I've secured you a manager's position in one of our smaller outlets in New Greentown."

"What!" exclaimed the man. "But there's nothing in New Greentown except for whores and body builders."

"Now listen, Bob, my wife comes from there!" Quick as a flash, Bob replied, "Really, Sir, body building's fascinating, did your wife win any prizes?"

To avoid being called up for active duty two men pulled all their teeth out before going in for their medical examination. On this particular morning there were just 3 of them – the two friends and a dirty looking tramp.

The first friend stood before the doctor and told him he had no teeth. The doctor put his finger in the man's mouth, ran it around his gums and agreed that he was not fit for active duty.

The doctor then turned to the tramp who told him he had very very painful piles.

"OK," said the doctor, "drop your trousers and turn round so that I can examine you."

The tramp did as he was told and the doctor stuck his finger up the man's arse and felt around.

"Mmm, they are bad," said the doctor. "You've failed the test as well."

He then turned to the second friend and said, "What's wrong with you?"

The man looked at the doctor's finger and shook his head vigorously.

"Nothing, nothing at all, doctor."

The Social Security said to Johnny, "Why don't you get a job?"

"What for?" he replied.

"So you can put some money in the bank until one day you'll have enough to retire and you can stop working."

"But I'm not working now," he retorted.

A big strapping boy went up to the big house for a job as a handyman but returned home very disappointed.

"Oh, dad, I'm so ashamed, I really made a cock up."

"How come, son?"

"The lady was very nice, she asked me lots of questions, seemed pleased with what I had to say, I told her I was a hard worker but then right at the end she asked to see my testimonials…that's when I lost it!"

A WALK ON THE WILD SIDE

The young man finally made up his mind to tell his mother he was gay. He could no longer keep it a secret so one evening when she was in the kitchen making supper, he took the plunge and told her.

"Mum, I have something to tell you, I'm gay."

Immediately, his mother replied, "Does being gay mean you have men's dicks in your mouth?"

"Well …" stammered the young man. "Yes, it does."

"In that case," she said angrily, "don't you ever criticise my cooking again."

A gay walks into a pub carrying a small bag and announces to the crowd, "If anyone can guess what's in my bag, I'm yours for the night."

A big, burly man stands up, thinking he'll have a laugh and shouts, "OK, I guess you've got a 10-ton truck in there."

The gay looks into his bag and smiles.

"Well done, we have a winner."

There was a convention on in town and all the available accommodation was taken up by the visiting delegates.

"I'm sorry, Sir, there isn't a room anywhere, the only bed I've got left means you'll have to share a room with one of our local residents and he snores so loudly you won't get any sleep at all." The weary traveller considered it for a moment and then smiled.

"No problem," he said, "I don't mind sharing."

The next morning, the man went to check out.

"Well, sir, you look well rested, you must have slept well, how did you manage it with all that snoring?"

"I wasn't disturbed at all," replied the man. "Before I went to sleep I blew the other man a kiss and said, 'Sleep well darling.' He stayed awake all night watching me."

A young man moves into a new neighbourhood, alone and without any friends. He's only been there a couple of days when there's knock on the door.

"Hi," says the visitor. "I'm Colin, I live just down the hall from you and I thought I'd come and introduce myself."

"Thanks," says the young man. "I'm Mike."

"Well Mike, would you like to come to a party over at my place on Saturday night? There'll be plenty of booze, great music and lots of sex."

"Wow, that sounds good, what do you reckon I should wear?" says Mike.

"Oh, come as you are, there'll only be the two of us."

★ ★ ★

Two retired gentlemen met up in their club for drinks. The first said, "How's that son of yours getting on, Bernard?"

"Oh, very well, thank you. This year his company made record profits so now he's bought himself a country estate. In fact, he's given away his flat in Mayfair to one of his friends. What about your son?" asked the second man.

"I'm pleased to say, he's also doing well. He's just finished a very successful film and with the proceeds, he's given away his 2-seater plane and bought himself a company jet."

As the two men sat there, contemplating their off-springs' good fortune, another man joined them.

"Good evening, Bernard, hello, Geoffrey, may I join you?"

"Certainly," they replied, "we were just catching up on news of our sons. How's yours doing, by the way?"

"Well, mixed fortunes really," he said. "Last week he confessed to my wife and I that he was gay. But it's not all bad news. He's made some lovely friends. One's given him a flat in Mayfair and the other's presented him with a 2-seater plane."

★ ★ ★

Alan and Cyril went to Blackpool for the weekend and because the weather was so hot, they decided to spend the afternoon on the beach. While Alan sunbathed, Cyril took the lilo into the water but after half an hour the wind suddenly blew up and he found himself floating out to sea.

Luckily, the lifeguards spotted the danger and took immediate action. A few minutes later, he was dragged gasping from the sea as Alan rushed up.

"Cyril, Cyril, are you alright? It's me, Alan."

"Indeed I'm not," gasped Cyril. "I was on that lilo for ages and not once did you look up and blow me a kiss."

"I'm sorry, dad, I think I've let you down."

"Why's that, son?"

"Yesterday we had to do our first parachute jump and when it came to my turn, I just froze, I couldn't make myself take that final step."

"So what happened?"

"The instructor told me if I didn't jump, he'd fuck me up the arse."

"So did you jump?"

"I did a little, at first."

One of the most beautiful girls in the region had all her clothes stolen when she went sunbathing in what she thought was a secluded spot. Realising that the evening was coming and it would get cold she knew she'd have to take a chance and get home as soon as possible.

At that moment she saw a young man pedalling along the road, flagged him down and told him of her plight. He readily agreed to take her home and she jumped on his bicycle. After 10 minutes she couldn't believe he wasn't affected by her appearance and said,

"Haven't you noticed I'm completely naked?"

"Oh yes," replied the young man, "but haven't you noticed that I'm riding a girl's bicycle?"

Two gay boys were having a terrible row.

"Fuck off," screamed the first.

"Go to hell," retorted the second.

"Kiss my arse," replied the first.

"Oh you want to make up now," smiled the second.

"Come in, Mr Flowers," said the doctor. "I've had the results of your tests and there's good news and bad news. The bad news is that you're a latent homosexual."

"Oh no," said the man aghast. "What's the good news?"

"Well the good news is that I find you very cute," replied the doctor.

"Paddy," asked the barmaid. "What are those two bulges in the front of your trousers?"

"I'll tell you what those are," replied Paddy heatedly. "They're two hand grenades and if that old queen comes up to me again and feels my balls, I'll blow his fucking fingers off."

LOVE AND MARRIAGE

As a young man, Johnny set his heart on a very special girl – a dream lover. But brewery heiresses who look like Marilyn Monroe, support Stoke City and drink pints, are very few and hard to find. Eventually, he took second best and married Marjorie, a 15-stone pub cleaner. Their wedding had a Wild West theme – well, her Dad brought a shotgun with him. A blissful marriage, they still have special pet names for each other. She calls him the Lone Ranger because he's always looking in her purse for silver, and he calls her Bubbles because her mouth's always covered in froth.

BEDTIME STORIES

She took him up to her bedroom and while he waited for her to slip into something more comfortable he noticed her room was piled high with all sorts of cuddly toys. But that was soon forgotten once they got down to it and made love. After it was over he turned to her and said smugly, "How was it for you?" "Not bad, I suppose," she replied, "you can pick anything from the bottom shelf."

"You look a bit down in the mouth mate, what's wrong?"
"T.h.e. w.e.d.d.i.n.g.'s o.f.f."
"No! what happened."
"I.f I t.a.l.k v.e.r.y s.l.o.w.l.y I d.o.n't s.t.a.m.m.e.r. a.n.y.m.o.r.e. S.o I w.a.s i.n t.h.e p.a.r.k w.i.t.h m.y f.i.a.n.c.é.e a.n.d w.e s.a.w a d.o.g s.c.r.a.t.c.h.i.n.g h.i.s b.a.c.k. I s.a.i.d w.h.e.n w.e w.e.r.e m.a.r.r.i.e.d s.h.e c.o.u.l.d d.o t.h.a.t f.o.r m.e a.n.d s.h.e s.t.o.r.m.e.d o.f.f."
"Why did she do that?"
"B.y t.h.e t.i.m.e I'd f.i.n.i.s.h.e.d s.p.e.a.k.i.n.g t.h.e d.o.g w.a.s l.i.c.k.i.n.g h.i.s b.a.l.l.s."

The two young lovers are in the back of the car parked in a quiet country lane.

"Julie," asks the man, "how about giving me some oral sex?"

"Oh no," she replies forcefully, "if I do that you'll never respect me again."

A year goes by and during that time he asks her for oral sex on a number of occasions but she always refuses. Eventually they get married and on the honeymoon night he asks her again for oral sex but she replies, "No, I know you'll never respect me again." Many years go by and the couple are now in their fifties. One day in bed the man turns to his wife and says, "Julie, after all these years of happily married life, a beautiful house, big car and two successful children, do you think we could have some oral sex? You know I will always respect you."

So at last the wife gives in and sometime later as they're relaxing in bed, the front doorbell chimes. He turns to her and says, "Hey cocksucker, answer that."

Always good for a chat up line, Johnny said to the girl, "Hello there sweetheart, fancy a bit of sex?"

"Definitely not," she retorted.

"Well, do you mind lying down while I do?" he replied.

Two girls boasting about their boyfriends.

"Jack's unbelievable," said the first girl. "He walks right up to me and puts it straight in."

"That's nothing," said the second girl.

"Bob puts it in and then walks straight up to me!"

A tom cat was running frantically about the base of the tree while a female cat was giving him the come on from one of the branches.

"Why don't you get up there and give her one," asked a fellow cat walking by.

"Listen, mate, have you ever tried climbing a tree with a hard on?."

The boastful man said to his girlfriend, "Darling, I'm going to fuck you so hard tonight you'll never forget it."

Later on in bed she turned to him and tapped him lightly on the head with a feather.

"What's that for?" he murmured.

"Well, I guess in comparative terms I'm beating you severely round the head!"

A young man met his match when he picked up a girl in a bar and took her back to his place. They were soon in bed doing the business – time and time again she called for more. After a couple of hours the poor bloke was knackered and to gain a short reprieve he said he had to go and put the car away for the night. Once inside the garage he thought he'd better inspect his poor overworked friend so he put his hand down his trousers but couldn't feel anything. In panic he pulled his trousers down and there it was all shrivelled up. He whispered gently to it, "It's all right, you can come out now, she's not here."

Did you hear about the arrogant man who was making love to his new girlfriend?
She whispered, "Please be careful, I have a weak heart."
"Nothing to worry about," he replied. "I'll be careful when I get up to the heart."

Jack went to the psychologist complaining of insomnia.
"Don't worry," came the reply, "just start at your toes and slowly relax all your body bit by bit and then you'll fall asleep."
That night Jack did as he was instructed.

"Go to sleep toes, go to sleep feet, go to sleep ankles, now you knees, go to sleep legs..."
But just at that moment his wife walked into the bedroom wearing the skimpiest and most sheer of nighties.
"Wake up everyone," he shouted.

A woman went to her vicar to seek advice on her forthcoming wedding. This was to be her third husband and she was not sure how to tell him that she was still a virgin.
"But how can that be?" exclaimed the vicar. "You've already had two husbands."
"That's true, but my first husband was a psychiatrist and all he did was talk about it, my second husband was a gynaecologist and all he did was look. But this time I'm sure it will be different. This time I'm marrying a lawyer so I'm sure to get screwed."

What's the similarity between Kodak and condoms?
They are both there to catch those special moments.

"Hello, hello, is that the vet?" said the distressed man. "Our dog has just swallowed a condom, what can I do?"
"Calm down, Sir, nothing to get too alarmed over, just keep

the dog rested and I'll be over after surgery."

Surgery ended and the vet decided to ring first.

"Hello, it's the vet here, how are things?"

"Oh everything's alright now," replied the man. "My girlfriend found another condom in the bathroom cabinet."

"Billy, I'm pregnant and if you don't marry me, I'll kill myself," wailed the girl.

"Oh June, you're a brick, not only are you a good fuck, but you're a good sport as well."

A young man asks for shelter for the night when his car breaks down in the middle of nowhere. The old couple invite him in, apologise for only having two bedrooms – one for them and the other for their unmarried daughter – but offer him the sofa for the night. Round about 4 am, it turns bitterly cold and the old woman comes down to see if he's alright.

"Would you like our eiderdown?" she asks.

"Oh no, no thank you!" he exclaims. "She's already been down twice."

A man is out on his first date with a woman who is sex mad. On the way home, she lures him into the park and urges him

to make love to her time and time again. Eventually, he's so knackered, he tells her he's just going to walk around and have a quiet smoke. As he does so, he bumps into a man coming home from the pub and he gets a great idea.

"Listen, mate," he says. "My girlfriend over there is so hot, she's worn me out. If I give you my gold watch, will you take over from me for a while?"

The man agrees and disappears into the dark undergrowth. Five minutes go by, when suddenly the park ranger appears and shines his torch on the passionate couple.

"Now what have we here?" he says.

"Just making love to my wife" comes the reply.

"Well, can't you do that at home?"

"But I didn't know it was my wife until you shone the torch on us."

A man comes home one night to find a nasty big rat humping a cat. The next day, he finds it humping a dog. Amazed at the sight, he takes the rat indoors to show his wife.

"Heh, Doris, you'll never believe what this rat…" but before he can finish, she interrupts him with a scream.

"Get that bloody sex maniac out of here."

93

"You look upset, Jack, what's wrong?"

"I've just found my wife in bed with my best friend."

"Oh mate, I'm sorry to hear that. What did you do?"

"I told her to pack her bags and fuck off."

"Good for you, and what about your best friend?"

"I got him by the scruff of the neck and said, 'Bad dog!'"

"How dare you ask me if I've been to bed with anyone else, that's my business," she said angrily.

"I'm sorry, I didn't know that was your profession," replied the young man.

Three dogs end up in the vet's and start talking to each other.

"Oh well," sighs the first, "this is it, they're going to put me down for worrying sheep."

"They're putting me down as well," says the second dog. "I bit the postman."

The two dogs turn to the third dog, a big Alsatian, and ask him why he is there.

"Well, it happened a couple of days ago. My beautiful blonde owner got out of the bath, bent down to dry her feet and I couldn't help myself. In a flash, I mounted her and went quite wild.

"I see," reply the other dogs, "so you're being put down as well."

"Oh no, I'm here to have my nails cut."

Taking a short cut home through the park one night, a spinster was confronted by a mugger.

"Give me all your money and jewellery," he demanded.

"But, I haven't got anything," she replied.

Not believing her, the man started to search her body. His hands moved everywhere, inside her blouse and up her skirt until he was satisfied she wasn't hiding anything. He was about to go when she said to him coyly, "Go on, keep trying, I can always write you a cheque."

The man was a prat. On his first date with a rather large lady, he commented arrogantly, "My dear, I have climbed some of the highest mountains in the world, but getting on top of you is going to be quite a challenge."

"Oh really!" she retorted. "I would have thought it all depended on the length of your rope."

All night long, the man had been bragging to his girl friend about his many talents, but when he said cheekily, "You know, it's a well-known fact that men with big dicks have small mouths", she finally exploded.

"So that explains it," she quickly replied, "because I could park a 10-ton truck in yours."

After chatting with his mates at work, the policeman comes home full of new ideas to make his sex life more exciting. When he sees his girlfriend he tells her of his new ideas.

"When I say Z Victor One to Sierra Oscar, you immediately run upstairs, strip off and jump into bed shouting 'help me, help me'. Then you shout Z Victor 2 to Sierra Oscar and I'll say 'Don't worry, I'm here to save you,' jump into bed and give you a good rogering."

So the next night, they put the plan into operation, but just as he's getting into the full rhythm, she suddenly shouts out "Z Victor 3 to Sierra Oscar." Startled, he stops and gasps, "What's that for?"

"That one means you'll have to change your truncheon because the one you've got doesn't seem to be having much effect," she replies.

"May I have 3 French letters please, Miss," asked the man in the chemist's shop.

The bitter old woman looked at him scornfully and replied, "Don't you Miss me, young man."

"Oh sorry," he replied "Make that 4 then, please."

"Do you want to liven up your love life?" one friend said to the other.

"If so, mount her from behind and whisper in her ear 'this is how I do it with your best friend.' Then I bet you can't stay on for more than 10 seconds."

Two sperm were swimming along when one said to the other, "How long do you reckon it'll take us to get there?"

"I think we've got quite a long way to go yet, we've only just passed the oesophagus."

"It's no good, it's over" said Julie. "You are so bad in bed."

"Oh come on," said the man affronted, "how can you tell after 15 seconds?"

A married couple and the husband's best friend go on holiday together and find they all have to share a bed in the

97

caravan. On the first night the husband falls asleep very quickly so the wife turns to the best friend and suggests they have a bit of fun.

"But what about your husband?" he whispers. "He's sure to wake up if we start anything like that."

"No, no," replies the wife, "he's dead to the world once he goes to sleep but if you're worried, pluck out one of his pubic hairs and see if he reacts."

So the best friend does as he is told and the husband remains snoring. Convinced all is well, the two get down to it and so enjoy themselves, they repeat it half a dozen times, pulling out one of the husband's pubic hairs each time to check he is still asleep. However, just as they are about to have sex a seventh time, the husband turns over and says, "Now hold on, mate, I don't mind you fucking my wife but I'm pissed off that you think you can keep score on my arse."

An emergency call was made to the local police station.

"Come quickly," gasped the voice, "a burglar is trapped in the bedroom of an old spinster."

"We'll be right there," said the desk sergeant. "May I ask who's talking?"

"It's me, the burglar, help!"

A female lecturer is telling a group of students how to teach maths to small children.

"It's always a good idea for them to visualise the question. For instance, if I said there were three cats on a wall and one was shot dead – how many were left? – the children would answer 2. They would be able to see the cats in their mind's eye."

At that point she was interrupted by one of the students.

"Excuse me, but I would have answered none to that question."

The lecturer looked puzzled, repeated the problem but again the student shook his head.

"My answer would be none," he said. "If one of the cats had been shot then the other two would have been out of there in a flash."

She replied, "Well, in theory that wouldn't be correct, however I like the way you think."

The student continued, "May I ask you a question now? If there were three women walking down the street, one licking an ice lolly, one biting an ice lolly and one sucking an ice lolly – which one would you think was married?"

The teacher blushed profusely and stuttered a reply.

"Well ... er ... the one sucking the ice lolly."

"No," replied the student, smiling, "it would be the one wearing a wedding ring ... still, I like the way you think!"

Two ducks meet in the hotel bar, have a few drinks and decide to book into a room for the night. But ever mindful of safe sex, they ask room service for a packet of condoms. A few minutes later the condoms arrive and the waiter asks, "Shall I put it on your bill, Sir?"

"Not bloody likely," bellows the male duck, "I'm not some kind of pervert you know."

A frustrated old spinster had read in a woman's magazine that the bigger the man's feet, the bigger his todger. This piece of information was still in her mind when two days later a tramp came to the door with the biggest feet she had ever seen. Quick as a flash, she invited him in and proceeded to wine and dine him before taking him up to bed. The next day as he was leaving she shouted at him crossly, "Next time, wear shoes that fit you."

For some years the lawyer had been taking his holidays at the exclusive hide-away country hotel and carrying on an affair with the owner's daughter. However, on returning one year he discovered his mistress had given birth to twin boys.

"Why on earth didn't you tell me?" said the astonished lawyer.

"You know I would have married you and provided for the birth."

She replied, "That may be so. But when I told my parents I was pregnant, we talked over all the options and decided it was far better to have a couple of bastards in the family than a lawyer.

The starry-eyed young man was boring his friend to death by continually going on about his beautiful young fiancée. Eventually, the friend could take it no more and blurted out, "I can't believe you really want to marry her, you must know she's been fucked by every man in town."
The young man thought hard for a moment or two and then replied defensively, "Okay, but this isn't really such a big town."

A young couple bought a parrot, but quickly discovered that he could cause them a lot of embarrassment. Every time someone came to the house, he would tell them what the couple had been up to, particularly what went on in the evenings on the sofa.
"That's it, I've had enough," said the man, "from now on, you'll be covered up early in the evening so you can't see what's going on. Otherwise, it's the zoo for you."
A few days later, the couple decided to go away for a week's holiday so they spent the evening packing and of course filled the suitcase to overflowing.

"I've got an idea," said the man. "I'll get on top, press down as much as I can and you can tell me what's happening." But the case wouldn't close.

"This is no good," remarked the wife.

"Here, let me have a go, I'll get on top and we'll see if it's any better."

Still they couldn't get the case to close, so the man said, "Let's both get on top, bounce up and down and maybe that'll work."

Suddenly the parrot pulled off the cage cover and squawked, "I'll take my chances at the zoo, but this I've just got to see?"

Bob's flat mate walked in to find his friend sitting on the sofa, both hands bandaged and a look of great distress on his face. "Bob, what's happened?" he gasped. "You look awful and you haven't been back all night."

"Oh Don, it's been a bloody nightmare," moaned Bob. "I've got to be the unluckiest bugger in the world. Last night, I went down the King's Arms and met this fabulous bird. She was really hot and it wasn't long before we were back at her place doing the business. All of a sudden, we heard a noise and she whispered frantically, "Quick, get out of here, it's my husband."

"You've never seen me move so quickly. I was straight out of bed and just managed to get through the window, hanging on the ledge by my fingertips, when he barged through the door. Bloody hell, Don, I was really in the shit. He crushed my fingers with a hammer and then closed the window on them. And if that wasn't enough, a passer-by reported me to the police for hanging there stark naked. Last night, I spent the time in police cells. You see how unlucky I was."

"Get away, Bob, it could happen to anyone," said Don, trying to console his distressed friend.

"But you don't understand," pleaded Bob. "When the cops arrested me, I discovered I was only 2 inches from the ground. Unlucky heh?"

The couple had been kissing and hugging on the sofa when Stan turned to Sal and whispered "How about it Sal, it's only a week until we get married, let's do it now."

"Oh no Stan" she replied. "We promised we wouldn't, can't you wait another seven days?"

Stan looked at her mournfully. "Okay Sal, but how about if you just give me a hint of what's to come. Go on Sal, unbutton your dress and let me have a quick feel of your beautiful breasts."

"Well alright" replied Sal and she did as he asked.

"Oooh Sal, that was wonderful. Will you just do one more thing for me. Will you let me have a sniff of your fanny?" So Sal relented, dropped her knickers and let Stan have a quick sniff.

"Oooh Sal" he said suddenly "are you sure it'll last another seven days?"

"There are three different stages of marriage" said Dad to his son on the boy's wedding day. "When you're newlyweds, you have sex wherever and whenever you want it – the house, the garden, in the supermarket, all over the place. But then comes stage 2. After you've been married for some time, sex is usually confined to the bedroom. And then comes stage 3. Many, many years on in a marriage, the most sex you get is when you pass each other on the stairs and say 'Fuck off!' "

A nymphomaniac could never find enough men to satisfy her so she decided to buy her own dildo. Now she had an old boyfriend who stocked some unique sexual aids and went along to ask him for something extra special." As it happens, I've just had this dildo delivered," he said. "It's from Hawaii and it's got strange powers. All you have to say is "Dildo fanny" and it will do the business."

So she took it home, unwrapped it and said "Dildo fanny" and the dildo jumped out of the box and up between her legs. It was the most fantastic feeling she'd ever had but when she wanted it to stop, it wouldn't. Her boyfriend hadn't given her the right words to say and she was now feeling very knackered.

"There's only one thing to do," she thought to herself. "I'd better get to the doctor's."

So she jumped in the car and drove as fast as she could to

the surgery but on the way a policeman stopped her for speeding. She explained her predicament, in between having another orgasm, but the policeman looked at her as if she was mad. "If I believed that, I'd believe anything," he said. "Dildo my ass!"

Julie was in bed waiting for her new lover to strip off. When he did, she was so amazed at the size of his todger, she jumped out of bed and rummaged in her handbag." What are you doing?" said the surprised man.
"I'm looking for a pencil, you've got to draw the line somewhere."

As the woman was walking down the street, she noticed a small boy who she thought was in need of a pee. Taking him by the hand she led him over to a little alley and helped him get his "winkie" out. but to her astonishment, it was huge and growing by the minute as she held it in her hand. "My goodness, young fellow, how old are you?"
"Twenty-eight" replied the jockey.

WEDDING BELLS

What do you say to a girl who can suck an olive through a straw? Will you marry me?

The young man was so nervous on meeting his future father-in-law that he blurted out, "Sir, may I have your daughter's hole in handy matrimony?"

Johnny looked around the church and turned to his best man, saying, "You know Jack, apart from my wife-to-be's two sisters, there's not a woman in this church that I haven't had."

Jack replied, "Well, in that case, between the two of us we've had them all."

There were some doubts about his wedding. On the great day his future father-in-law said to the vicar, "Why do you rope off the aisles?"

"So the groom can't get away," replied the vicar.

★ ★ ★

Chuck and Jan arrived at the Registry Office to fill in the forms required for their wedding in two weeks' time. As Chuck wrote his name, the clerk told him he could not accept a nickname. He had better go next door to the Births, Deaths and Marriages Department to check out his full Christian name. So Chuck went next door and a few minutes later came back and duly filled in his name as Charles. But then it was Jan's turn and she was also told to go next door and confirm her full name. In this case it was Janette.

"It's a good thing I'm thorough," said the clerk smugly, "or this marriage wouldn't have been legal and any kids you might have had would be technical bastards."

"What a coincidence," said Jan, "that's exactly what the bloke next door said about you."

★ ★ ★

HONEYMOONING

It was seven days into their honeymoon and the young bride staggered downstairs to breakfast looking knackered.

"My goodness," said the waitress. "You don't look so good, but aren't you the bride with the older husband?"

"Yes I am, he's 75, but I've discovered he's pulled a dreadful trick on me. When he told me he had saved up for 50 years, I thought he was talking about money."

Two friends talking over the garden wall.

"Did you do as I suggested?" said Doreen. "Did you feed him a dozen oysters on your honeymoon night?"

"Oh I did," replied the other, "but only 10 of them worked!"

"You'll never believe this, Johnny," said the simple friend. "My wife's a bit backward. Why! on our wedding night she put the pillow under her arse instead of her head."

Two couples got married on the same day and ended up in the same hotel for their honeymoon. One evening, the girls having already gone to bed, the two men had a couple of drinks together in the bar. As time went on the men started to get boastful and Geoff claimed he could make love to his wife more times than John.

Fired up with booze, John accepted the challenge and they agreed to meet the following morning with the results.

"Last night, I made love to my wife 3 times" said Geoff at breakfast time. "What about you?"

John replied, "34 times."

"What!!" exclaimed Geoff. "OK, double or nothing, let's see what happens tonight."

The next day Geoff arrived in the dining room looking knackered.

"7 times," he said to John.

John laughed. "You lose again, 48 times for me."

"Well that's unbelievable, how do you manage it?"

"Listen, I'll show you. Put your hips back, then push forward quickly. That's one. Now, pull your hips back again and push forward quickly. That's two…"

Jack and Sally were re-tracing their steps and visiting all the places they saw on their honeymoon, 30 years previously.

"Look, Sal, isn't that the little stream we paddled in, and over there…do you remember I sat you on that wall and we made love? Come on, let's do it again."

So he put Sally on the fence and they got down to business, but this time Sally went absolutely wild.

"Gosh, Sal, that was incredible, you didn't do that last time we were here."

"No," she replied, "but back then, the fence wasn't electrified."

A middle-aged man and a young girl had just got married and were now in the honeymoon suite. The man took his trousers off, handed them to his new wife and said, "Here, put these on."

Puzzled, the girl replied, "But these won't fit me."

"That's right," he said. "I just wanted to be sure that you knew who would be wearing the trousers in this marriage."

"Oh really!" she sneered, as she took off her knickers and threw them at him.

"Put these on," she said.

"Don't be silly, I can't get into these."

She replied, "Too bloody right you can't and you never will if you start spouting those old fashioned ideas at me."

The new husband and wife were having a last drink in the bar before retiring to the honeymoon suite.

"I'll go up and get ready," smiled the wife and she went upstairs. Ten minutes later, her husband followed, but when he walked into the room, he found his wife in bed with the hotel porter and a male guest from across the corridor.

"What's going on here?" he spluttered.

"Oh don't look so surprised, darling," she said. "I always told you I could never say no to a party."

A man marries a young naive country girl and on their wedding night, he shows her his tackle and tells her he's the only man to have such a thing. Times goes by and after a couple of months, they're in bed one morning when she grabs his willy and remarks, "You were fibbing when you told me you were the only man to have one of these, I've discovered that Mr Biggun across the road has one as well." The husband thinks quickly and replies, "Oh yes, that was a spare one I had, so I gave it to him.", "Oh darling," she sighs.

"Why did you give him the best one?"

The Reverend James and his newly married wife retire to the honeymoon suite, where she gets ready for bed and he disappears into the bathroom. A few minutes later he comes out to find his wife is already under the covers.

"Doris, I thought I'd find you on your knees," he said.

"Oh darling, we can do it that way another time, for the moment I'd like to see your face."

111

The morning after their honeymoon night the husband comes down to breakfast to see just a piece of lettuce and a carrot on his plate.

"What's this?" he asks.

She replies, "I just want to know if you eat like a rabbit too."

After a wonderful honeymoon night, the new husband wakes to find his wife in tears.

"Darling, what's wrong? Was it too much for you last night?"

"Oh no, no," sobbed the wife, "but look at it this morning, I fear we've used it all up."

It was love at first sight. Within a week of meeting, John and Mary decided to get married.

"But we don't really know anything about each other," said Mary.

"Never mind," replied John. "We'll learn as we go along."

So the couple got married and went to Spain for their honeymoon where they spent a blissful few days until one morning as they were sunbathing around the pool.

John suddenly got up, climbed to the very top of the diving board and performed a very intricate dive involving back flips and a double pike.

"Wow!" said Jane, when he returned. "That was truly amazing!"

"Well, I used to be the British Diving Champion," replied John. "You see, didn't I say we'd find out more about each other as time went by?"

A little later, Jane got up, dived into the pool and swam four lengths without stopping.

"Heh!" said John, much impressed, that was fantastic. "Were you in the British Squad?"

"Oh no," she replied. "I spent a few years in Venice where I was on the game and my patch included both sides of the canal."

The bride was in floods of tears. Only an hour before her wedding and the heel had broken on her new shoes.

"Don't worry," said the bridesmaid. "I've got a pair of white shoes, they may be a bit small but I think you'll be able to put up with them for a short while."

So the wedding went ahead without mishap and afterwards at the reception there was much merrymaking. However, by the end of the evening, Megan's feet were in agony and she couldn't wait to get upstairs to their honeymoon suite to get the shoes off.

Unbeknown to the happy couple, some of the guests, including the parents, followed them upstairs to listen outside the door. For a few minutes they giggled as they heard the sound of huffing and puffing and groaning and then the bridegroom was heard to say, "My goodness Megan, that was tight."

"There!" whispered her mother. "I told you she was a virgin."
But then they all got quite a surprise when they heard him say,

"Okay, now for the other one."

Again, there was the sound of groaning and panting until the bridegroom spoke again.

"Blimey, that was even tighter."

"Good lad," whispered his father.

"Once a sailor, always a sailor."

MARRIED BLISS

A man shouted to his wife, "Lisa, come here a minute and have a look at my grandfather clock."
Lisa walks in to find her husband with his trousers round his ankles and his dick standing to attention.
"What are you playing at?" she demands. "That's no grandfather clock."
"It will be when you put two hands and a face on it," he replied.

It's late at night and the husband and wife are in bed. She's just about to fall asleep when he whispers in her ear.
"How about a little loving then?"
"Oh no," she replies. "I have to see the gynaecologist tomorrow so I don't want any foreign bodies."
A couple of minutes go by and he nudges her again, saying, "You don't have a dentist appointment tomorrow, do you?"

Did you hear about the man who had "I love you" tattooed on his dick?
That night in bed, he turned to his wife and said, "What do you think of this, Sal?"

115

"There you go," she exclaimed, "always trying to put words in my mouth."

"Come on, Josie," said Jack. "Let's have an early night, I've got a full head of steam here."

Josie wasn't too willing but in the end agreed and they went up to bed. Josie put on a long nightdress.

"Come on, Josie, take that nightgown off," pleaded Jack but just at that moment the phone went and Jack went down to answer it. Quick as a flash, Josie barricaded the door and jumped into bed. When Jack returned and found he couldn't get in, he yelled with anger.

"Come on, Josie, let me in or I'll break the door down."

"Oh yeah," sneered Josi?", "You and who else. You can't even manage to take a nightgown off and here you are threatening to break down a door!"

Adam was all alone in the Garden of Eden and as he was wandering about he came across two rabbits, one humping the other.

"What are those two rabbits doing?" he asked the Lord.

And the Lord replied, "They are making love."

A little later he came across two doves, one mounted on the other.

"Lord, what are those two birds doing?" asked Adam.

116

"They are making love" came the reply.

Adam thought for a moment and then said, "Why am I all alone?

Why don't I have someone to love?"

"OK, Adam, when you wake up in the morning, you won't be alone any longer."

So the next day when Adam awoke, Eve was lying next to him.

He immediately jumped on top of her but a moment later he asked, "Lord, what's a headache?"

A young couple had been married for less than six months but the bride was obsessed with knowing how many women her husband had slept with.

"If I tell you, it'll only make you angry and upset" he said.

"No it won't," she assured him. "I just need to know."

Eventually the man gave in.

"OK, now let's see. One...two...three...four...five...six... seven...eight...you...ten...eleven..."

Pam is at the end of her tether. Her husband is out of work and all he does is sit or lie in front of the TV drinking beer. One day, the washing machine breaks down and she asks him to take a look at it.

"Leave it out," he says. "Who do you think I am, a washing

machine expert?"

As luck would have it, later on in the day the vacuum cleaner packs up and again she asks him if he would have a look at it."

"Don't be daft, woman, do I look like an electrician? Now leave me in peace."

And because things always come in threes, next morning the back door gets stuck and won't open. Feeling very fed up, she confronts her idle husband and tells him about the door.

"Bugger off," he replies, "do I look like a chippie?"

That's it. She's had enough. She gets three different tradesmen in and all is repaired. In the evening, when she tells her husband about the repairs, he asks her how much the damn thing is going to cost.

"Well, they told me I could either pay by baking a cake or having sex," she replies.

"So what cake did you bake?"

"Don't be silly," she says scornfully. "Do I look like Mrs Beeton?"

Two astronauts successfully landed on the moon and transmitted their thoughts and feelings back to mission control. They described the moon's surface, the temperature, the atmosphere and their own feelings of elation at being there. Just as transmission was going off, one of the astronauts was heard to say, "Good luck Mr Collins". When the men eventually returned to earth there was a lot of media attention but when it came to the meaning of "Good luck Mr Collins", the astronaut refused to explain.

Twenty-five years later, on the anniversary of the moon landing, once again the two astronauts become the centre of attention. It was then, on a late night television programme that the meaning of "Good luck Mr Collins" was finally revealed.

"When I was a young boy, our family lived next door to Mr and Mrs Collins," he began, "and one day when I was playing in the garden I heard voices coming from their open bedroom window. I heard Mrs Collins yelling at her husband, 'Oral sex, that's what you want, is it ... oral sex? Let me tell you, when the boy next door lands on the moon, then you'll get oral sex!' "

A couple were in bed. The wife had turned over to go to sleep but the man decided to read. After a minute he stopped, put his hand between his wife's legs and fondled her. Then he stopped and went back to reading his book. As he did so, his wife turned round, sat up and took off her nightdress.

"What are you doing that for?" asked her husband.

"Well, after what you've just done, I thought you were keen for some sex."

"Oh no, not at all," he replied.

"Then why were you playing with my pussy?"

"I couldn't turn the pages of my book," he said.

★ ★ ★

A woman comes home to find her husband crying his eyes out.

"My goodness, what's wrong?" she asks.

He looks up at her and says, "Do you remember 15 years ago when I got you pregnant? Your father was so flamin' angry he said I had to marry you or go to jail?"

"Yes, I remember," she replies, "but why are you thinking of that now?"

"Well, today is the day I would have been released!"

A couple are having marital problems and go along to see the marriage counsellor.

"Eternal triangle problem, is it?" asked the counsellor. "Don't worry, we can solve that. Why! it even happened to my marriage once."

"Really," replied the couple, "what did you do?"

"We ate the sheep."

"My wife should be a goalie, she'd be the best," said one man to his friend.

"Why's that?"

"I haven't scored for months."

The poor insignificant little man was confronted by his overpowering wife as he got ready for bed.

"If you can guess what I've got behind my back, I'll reward you with a night of passion," she bellowed.

Paling at the thought, he replied, "A double decker bus."

"Not quite," she laughed, "but it'll do."

As the motorcyclist drew up to the traffic lights, a car screeched to a halt and a man jumped out and ran up to him.

"For goodness sake man, didn't you realise your wife had fallen off when you took that sharp bend a mile back?"

"Oh thanks, mate," replied the happy motorcyclist. "For a moment I thought I'd gone deaf."

A lively young girl married a shy retiring man and after one week of marriage he came home from work looking very puzzled.

"When I got to the office this morning I found a pencil tied to my penis."

"That's right, my love," she replied. "I decided that if you couldn't come at least you could write."

121

Although divorced five years previously, the couple had remained friends for the sake of their daughter. One day, the ex-wife learns that her ex-husband has been taken ill and will have to stay in bed for at least two weeks. Because he's on his own, she decides to go round to see if there's any way she can help and she volunteers to take over from the nurse who has been popping in for an hour each day. The ex-wife learns to give him his medicines, cook his food and generally look after him. One day, she's giving him a bed bath when she notices he has a huge erection.

"Oh my goodness," she remarks. "Look, John, he still remembers me."

Two men were sitting in a bar talking.

"John, I've got a big favour to ask you. I've got to go away for a few days to the firm's headquarters in Leeds and my wife will be here on her own. Although I try not to, I can't help being suspicious that something is going on. Would you mind just keeping an eye on her while I'm gone?"

His friend agrees and it's more than two weeks later that they meet up again, on his return.

"Anything to report, John?" asks the suspicious husband.

John replies hesitantly, "Well, I watched your wife every evening and on the third night, a man arrived in a sports car. They sat and had cocktails on your patio, then went skinny dipping in the pool before going inside and upstairs. They kissed passionately and he laid her down on the bed but

then he closed the curtains so I didn't see any more."
"You see," says the husband sadly. "There's still no proof, only suspicions."

"Mrs Smith, I have some very bad news for you, concerning your husband, We've had the tests back and it shows that he has only hours to live. I'm afraid he'll probably be dead by tomorrow morning."
The poor woman goes home in a terrible state of shock but she is determined to make his last few hours the best he's ever had. That night, she suggests they go upstairs early and wearing her most sexiest nightie, she lures him into bed and makes love to him like he's never experienced before. After 2 hours, they lay back exhausted and fall asleep. But half an hour later, the husband wakes up, nudges his wife and tells her it was so wonderful, can they do it again. Now this happens all night long until the poor wife hardly has the strength to move. As dawn breaks, he whispers yet again, "Just once more, darling, please," and in a sudden flash of anger she replies, "It's alright for you. You don't have to get up in the morning."

The couple had been married for many years and all romance had gone out of their marriage. One day, as his wife was getting ready for bed, he grabbed her boobs and her bum, saying, "If these were firmer you wouldn't need so much scaffolding!"

The wife was very upset and the next day when the husband stripped off to have a shower, she grabbed hold of his todger and said, "If this was firmer, I wouldn't need the man next door."

"Cath," said Fred. "I don't know too much about this sex thing, I guess we'll have to go and see the doctor."

So the newlyweds visited the surgery and asked the doctor to show them how it was done. The doctor agreed, told Cath to take all her clothes off and then he got down on top of her and performed enthusiastically. When it was over he said, "That's what sex is, now do you understand?"

"Yes, thank you, doctor," said Fred, "and how often do I have to bring her in to see you?"

"Oh my darling, drink makes you look so sexy."

"But I haven't been drinking."

"No, but I have."

A woman returned from the doctor's to find her husband sprawled in a chair.

"Why are you so happy?" he moaned, looking at her smiling face.

"I've just been told that I have the breasts of an 18-year-old."

"Really! and what did he say about your 50 year old arse?"

"We didn't talk about you," she replied.

The young couple arrived back from a wonderful honeymoon to begin their married life in a little terraced cottage. After his first day back at work, the husband returned home to find his wife in floods of tears.

"What's wrong, darling?" he asked.

"Oh Ben, I wanted everything to be so perfect for you, but I've gone and burnt the dinner."

The man took her in his arms, consoled her and they ended up in bed. The next day, he arrived home to discover the dinner had been spoilt again, so after comforting her, they ended up in bed a second time. This continued all week but when he arrived home on Friday night, instead of seeing her in tears, he found her sliding down the bannister stark naked.

"What are you doing?" he exclaimed.

"I'm just keeping your dinner warm," she replied.

Coming home from work earlier than planned, the husband found his wife in the kitchen, bending over the oven. She looked so desirable, he immediately dropped his trousers and took her from behind. After it was finished, he gave her a sharp smack on the bum.

"What the bloody hell was that for?" she raged.

"That was because you didn't look round to see who it was," he exclaimed.

Watching his wife put her bra on, the man sneered, "I don't know why you bother, it's not as if you've got anything to put in it."

"Bugger off," she replied. "I don't complain when I'm ironing your underpants."

"Are you happy, darling?" asks the man after six months of marriage.

"Of course, I'm very happy," she replies.

"But there is something that bothers you, isn't there?" he persists.

"Well…er…it's just that you're always picking your nose and you're always on top when we make love."

"Let me explain," he says. "When I was growing up, my father used to say to me quite often, 'Whatever you do, keep your nose clean and don't fuck up.' "

"You know, Bob, I don't know how much longer I can stand it. My wife is just a dirty good-for-nothing. The house is a tip, she never cooks and the whole place is filthy. I've just got to get rid of her."

"Listen, Steve, I've got an idea," said his mate. I read somewhere that people can die from having too much sex. Why don't you spend the whole weekend in bed with her and see what happens." So Steve followed Bob's advice and spent the whole weekend in bed. On Monday morning, he was so knackered he could barely get himself to work. That night, he arrived home to find out how successful the plan had been, but as he walked in, he couldn't believe his eyes. The house was gleaming, everything was spotlessly clean and a roast was cooking in the oven. Standing in the kitchen with a glass of champagne in her hand was his wife in a sexy négligé.

"You see, lover," she said, smiling. "You do right by me and I'll do right by you."

A woman was so desperate for a husband, she advertised for one in the local newspaper. The next day, she got over 500 replies from women saying, "You can have mine."

A woman went to the doctor's complaining of a total lack of energy. After being examined, he told her she was on the edge of a nervous breakdown and should give up cigarettes, gin and sex for 3 months. But after a week, the woman returned saying she was even closer to a breakdown if she couldn't smoke."

"OK, have 5 cigarettes a day."

Another week went by and she returned saying she missed her glass of gin so much, it helped to relax her.

"OK, just one glass a day," said the doctor.

Two weeks later she returned again and before she could say anything, the doctor quickly interrupted.

"OK, OK, but only with your husband – there must be no excitement."

★　★　★

"Doctor, doctor," said the frustrated woman. "How can I improve my husband's performance in bed?"

"Well, first of all, you must tell him what you want," suggested the doctor.

So in bed that night, the wife turned towards her husband and whispered, "Darling, caress my breasts and tell me how much you love me."

So the husband did as she asked.

Then, she whispered again, "Lower."

So in a very deep voice he said, "I love you."

In the middle of the night, the woman nudged her husband saying, "Jack, I think I heard a noise downstairs. Are you awake?"

"No," he replied.

★ ★ ★

A man sat at the end of the bar looking sadly into his pint of beer.

"You don't look so good, Bob. What's wrong?" asked the barman.

"It's the bloody wife," he moaned. "She makes my life so miserable, nag, nag, nag, all the time."

"Well, I've got a bit of advice," offered the barman. "There was a fellow in here not long ago who had the same problem and he was told that if he made love to his wife for five hours every night, she wouldn't be able to take the strain and within two months, she'd be dead."

"Was she?" asked Bob, with interest.

"You bet she was," replied the barman. So Bob went home and for the next six weeks he made love to his wife every night for five hours. One evening, he staggered into the bar looking 10 years older and completely knackered.

"How's it going?" asked the barman, looking concerned.

"Well, the wife may be smiling a lot more and enjoying life to the full, but I console myself with the knowledge that she's only got two more weeks to live."

★ ★ ★

The event made headline news in the local paper.

"Man of 80 marries girl of 21."

The man was in such great demand that it was arranged for him to hold a press conference when they returned from their honeymoon.

"How often do you have sex?" shouted out one of the journalists.

"Nearly every night," replied the man.

"Nearly on Monday, nearly on Tuesday, nearly on Wednesday …"

★ ★ ★

A rich old man of 85 went to the doctor's for a check-up. He explained that he was about to get married to a young girl of 20 and he needed to know how fit he was.

"Well, for a man of your age, you are remarkably well, but," cautioned the doctor, "are you sure you're doing the right thing? It may well put a lot of strain on you."

But the old man could not be persuaded to change his mind.

"Well, in that case," persisted the doctor, "it may be a good idea to take in a lodger. I'm sure you will find the marriage a lot less strenuous."

The old man thought this over and said it sounded like a good idea. A few months later the doctor and the old man met up again at the village fete.

"Hello, doctor," beamed the old man, "you must

congratulate me, my wife is pregnant."
The doctor kept a straight face, as he wished the old man well.
"I guess you took my advice about taking in a lodger then?"
"Indeed I did," winked the old man, enjoying himself", and she's pregnant too!"

A young couple move to a remote island off the coast of Newfoundland. They are made very welcome by the locals although the husband is teased a great deal because he is clean shaven. All the other men on the island have long beards. One night, as the couple are getting ready for bed, he has an idea. When his wife has undressed, he asks her to do a handstand in front of the mirror. Thinking it very odd, but curious to know what he's going to do, she agrees. Then the husband puts his face between her legs and murmurs to himself. "Okay, maybe a beard won't be so bad after all.

The marriage was going through a rocky patch; even though Christmas was approaching, there was very little goodwill.
"Why you old skinflint," exclaimed Doris. "You haven't even bought me a present."
"Why should I," Bob retorted. "I bought you a plot in the cemetery last year and you still haven't used it!"

A man, his wife and daughter are arguing about who should pop down the shops for a pint of milk. "I'll tell you what," says the man finally. "Whoever speaks first has to go and get the milk." The others agree and silence ensues.

Ten minutes later, the girl's boyfriend walks in. "Hello everyone," he says, but there is no response. "How about a cup of tea?" Still no one speaks, so he goes over to his girlfriend, gives her a lip smacking kiss and leads her out of the door and up the stairs. Half an hour later he returns looking a little flushed but still no one speaks. He decides to have a bit of fun so he goes up to the wife and gives her a kiss. He can't believe she doesn't say anything, so he takes this as a "yes" and takes her upstairs as well. Twenty minutes later he returns feeling quite knackered. As he passes the mirror he catches sight of his bedraggled appearance and his hair which is now sticking up in the air. Needing to tidy up, he asks, "Anyone got any vaseline?"

At that, the man jumps up from his chair and rushes to the door. "You're right," he says, "a cup of tea would be nice, I'll just pop out for the milk."

A vicious burglar breaks into a house late at night, orders the couple out of bed and ties them up. Now the husband is a big sissy, afraid of his own shadow, so he whispers to his wife, "Darling, do whatever he says. If he wants sex with you,

then let him have it, otherwise he might hurt us."
"Whatever you say," replies his wife. "By the way, he told me
he thought you had a nice, tight little bum."

A husband and wife booked into an hotel only to find their
room had two single beds. In the middle of the night, the
husband whispered over, "Oh darling, sweetheart, how
about coming over here so I can make love to my beautiful
wife."
The wife slipped out of bed, but as she crept over to him, she
knocked the bedside table and upset a glass of water.
"Never mind, darling," he cooed, "it's not your fault, it's just
too dark in here."
After a passionate session, the wife returned to her own bed
but on the way back she hit the bedside table again and
knocked over the lamp."
"Watch out, you stupid bitch, you're so bloody clumsy," he
yelled.

NEST BUILDING

For a man who spent so much of his youth on the nest, having to build one came as a bit of a shock. As newly-weds, he and Marjorie had their first house, a back-to-back, in Gas House Lane. Mind you, decorating wasn't his forte, he thought D.I.Y. stood for "Drink It Yourself". He was a poor handyman, he got the putty mixed up with the vaseline and his windows fell out. After only six months, Johnny and Marjorie's bedroom fluttered and echoed to the delightful patter of tiny feet. Well, he had to have somewhere to keep the pigeons after the loft blew down! Johnny was eventually arrested for being a Peeping Tom, after misunderstanding the meaning of Neighbourhood Watch.

CHURCH TIMES

It was Saturday night and Ted and his two mates were all dressed up ready to paint the town red. But first, as usual, Ted popped into church for confession.

"Forgive me Father, for I have sinned. I slept with a woman who was not my wife."

"I suppose it was Mary from the dairy."

"No, Father."

"Don't tell me it was Beth at the Kings Arms?"

"No, Father."

"Then it must have been that brazen hussy from the newsagent's?"

After the priest had given out the penance, Ted went back outside to meet his friends. He smiled at them, saying,

"It's worked again, lads, I've got the names of another three ravers!"

The young priest was about to hear his first confession. Sitting further away was the old priest to keep an eye on him. After it was over, the young priest asked how he had done. "Not too bad," replied the old priest. "Just make sure you don't say really! never! core! and wow! so much in future. Stick to more tut tuts."

A vicar went into a pet shop to buy something that would keep him company.

"I've got just what you need," said the pet shop owner. "Take a look at this parrot. Not only does it talk but if you pull the string on his left leg he'll sing 'Rock of Ages' and if you pull the string on his right leg, he'll recite the Lord's Prayer."

"That is truly remarkable," exclaimed the vicar, "but what happens if I pull both strings at the same time?"

"I fall off my bloody perch, you wanker," screeched the parrot.

A simple-minded man was sitting opposite a priest on the train.

"Excuse me, why do you wear your collar back to front?" asked the man.

"It's because I'm a Father," replied the priest.

"But I'm a father too," said the man, "and I don't wear my collar back to front."

"Aah, but the difference is, I'm a father to thousands."

"Well, in that case," retorted the man, "it's not your collar, it's your trousers you should wear back to front."

The local priest rang up his oppo in the Church of England asking him for a favour.

"I'm supposed to hear confessions in half an hour but something unexpected has come up and I have to be the other side of the diocese by 2 o'clock. Will you take over from me here?" asked the priest.

"What! but I've never done it before."

"It's quite straight forward" said the priest. "Sit in with me for half an hour before I go and you'll soon get the hang of it."

So the vicar agrees and is soon hidden away within earshot of the confessional. The first person to enter is a woman.

"Father, I have sinned."

"What have you done my child?"

"I have been unfaithful."

"How many times have you been unfaithful?"

"Four times Father and I am truly sorry."

"Very well, Put £2 in the box and say 10 Hail Mary's and you'll be absolved."

Not long after another woman comes in.

"Father, I have sinned."

"What have you done my child?"

"I have slept with a married man."

"How many times?"

"Twice."

"Then put £1 in the box, say 5 Hail Mary's and you'll be absolved."

Moments later the priest whispered to the vicar. "You see how it works? Take over from me now, I have to go."

So the vicar seated himself comfortably in the confessional and immediately a woman sat down on the other side.

"Father, I have sinned," she said.

"What have you done, my child?"

"I have committed adultery."

"How many times?"

"Only once, Father."

"Well, you'd better go back and do it again."

"What! You want me to do it again?"

"Yes, it's two for £1."

"Hello Bob, how did you get that black eye?" asked John. "In church. As we stood up to sing, a large lady in front of me had her dress stuck in the cheeks of her bum, so I pulled it out but all I got in the way of thanks was a black eye."

The following week the two men met again and John was amazed to see Bob had now got two black eyes.

"Don't tell me you got the other black eye in church as well?" he said.

"Well that I did" said Bob. "I was in church with my son and when we got up to sing, the same woman had her dress stuck in the cheeks of her bum. Before I could stop him, my son had pulled the dress out. Now I know she didn't like that so I put it back in … and that's when she hit me."

Mother Superior was talking to one of her young nuns.

"Sister, if you were out late at night on your own and a man attacked you, what would you do?"

"I would lift up my habit" she replied.

"Goodness me, and then what would you do?"

"I would tell him to drop his pants."

"Oh, Lord! Save us!" uttered the shocked Mother Superior. "And then what?"

"I would run away as fast as I could, and I can run much faster with my habit up, than he can with his trousers down."

★ ★ ★

A man goes into the confessional and says.

"Forgive me Father for I have sinned. Yesterday, I cursed badly, using the F-word."

"Why was that?" asked the priest.

"I was playing a round of golf, all was going well until I reached the 10th hole when my T-shot ended up in thick undergrowth."

"Is that when you said the F-word?"

"No, I stayed calm, took my time and hit a clean shot out of the rough, down the fairway but at the last moment it hit a small branch and veered off into the bunker."

"I like a game of golf myself" said the priest "that really is so annoying, was that when you used the F-word?"

"No, I tried not to let it get to me. I took my time and hit a beautiful ball up onto the green only 2 inches from the hole."

"How frustrating, is that when you used the F-word?"

"No Father, I still remained calm…"

"Don't tell me!" interrupted the priest, "You didn't miss the fucking putt!!"

"Come in George," said the Mother Superior to her gardener. "I hear you've got a complaint."

"That I have," he replied, "one of your nuns has been doing press-ups in my vegetable garden."

"Well surely there's no harm in that."

"Aah, but you've not seen my cucumbers, they're all ruined."

A young girl went into confession and told the priest she had slept with four different men over the past week. Jack on Tuesday, Bill on Wednesday, Peter on Thursday and Chuck on Friday.

"Well my child" said the priest "on your way home tonight buy two lemons and suck on them."

"But Father, will that cleanse me of my sins?" she asked.

"No, but it'll take that bloody damned smile off your face."

Two nuns were walking back to the convent late at night when they saw a suspicious man coming towards them.

"Quick" whispered one of the nuns. "Show him your cross and he may leave us alone."

"Good idea," replied the other and raising her voice as loud as possible she said angrily "Fuck off, you little bastard."

A drunk staggers into church and wanders up the aisle moaning to himself.

"Help me, help me, it's bloody agony."

Eventually, he makes it into the confessional and all goes quiet. After a few minutes the priest decides he'd better find out if everything is alright so he says, "May I help you my son?"

"I don't know" comes the reply, "it depends on whether you have any paper in there."

In fact the story of Adam and Eve has become slightly mistold over the years. As it happens, Eve was created first and God gave her three breasts. But after a while she complained that she was in some pain because they kept bumping against each other, so he agreed to take the middle one away. Time passed and Eve began to get bored so she asked God if he could make her someone to play with.

"Of course" replied God. "I'll call him man ... now where did I put that useless tit?"

The vicar knocked at the door and a boy of 14 answered, beer in one hand, a cigarette dangling from his mouth and girls hanging off his arms.

"Excuse me son" said the vicar somewhat taken aback "is your mum or dad in?"

"Fuck off" sneered the boy "does it look like it?"

Three nuns went to confession.

"Forgive me Father for I have sinned," said the first nun, "I looked at a man's penis."

"Then wash your eyes with holy water," said the priest.

In came the second nun.

"Forgive me Father for I have sinned. I touched a man's penis."

"Then go and wash your hands in holy water," came the reply. The third nun went in and it was some time before she reappeared and joined her colleagues.

"Sorry I was so long," she said, "I just had to go and gargle."

A new vicar had taken over at the small village church of St Gregory and he was eager to make a good impression. After the service, the congregation emerged from the church and each shook hands with the vicar.

"Lovely sermon," said one.

"It really made me stop and think," said another.

All of a sudden, a rather scruffy man appeared and as he shuffled past he mumbled, "Load of bollocks."

Determined not to be affected by this, the vicar carried on

greeting his parishioners.

"Splendid sermon," they said, "thank you very much".

"Quite inspiring."

The vicar beamed gratefully.

"Absolute crap, call himself a vicar?" came the mumbling of the scruffy man as he passed the vicar again. This time, the vicar was more upset and the situation worsened as the man kept appearing and making comments.

"Bored to tears", "not worth listening to", "what a prat!" The vicar could take it no longer. He turned to one of the congregation and pointed out the scruffy man.

"Oh, you mustn't worry about old Ned, Vicar," said a kindly old woman.

"He's not right in the head, he just goes around repeating what everyone else has said."

"Oh Father, Father," said the distressed woman to her parish priest. "How would you tackle a serious drink problem?"

"With a corkscrew," came the reply.

A popular local dignitary had died and the church was full to overflowing with people who had come to pay their last respects. At the front of the church stood the coffin and just as the funeral service was about to start, an escaped lunatic jumped on top of it and started pulling at the clasp.

Immediately, one of the family hurried over and urged him to get down. But he refused to move.

"Look, I'll give you £20 to get off," said the man desperately but still the lunatic refused to move. Another member of the family came over and offered him £40. The lunatic shook his head. A third member came over and shouted, "Here, you can have £100."

"No," said the lunatic confidently. "I'll open the box."

Once a month, the vicar goes on a tour of his outlying parish and as he's walking up the lane to one of the more remote farms he sees the farmer in a field shagging a goat. Averting his eyes he continues on and spots the farmer's son behind the haystack being intimate with a sheep.

Then, just as he gets to the farmyard he catches sight of the old grandfather masturbating. Unable to control his disgust, the vicar marches up to the front door and knocks loudly.

"Oh, good morning, Vicar," says the farmer's wife, "this is a nice surprise."

"Surprise my foot," splutters the vicar. "I've just seen your husband shagging a goat, your son fucking a sheep and your grandfather having a wank."

"Yes, I know, its very sad," she says, "but you see, grandpa's too old to go chasing the animals anymore."

Two nuns are cycling down a narrow cobblestone street when one says to the other, "I haven't come this way before." "Neither have I, it's the cobbles you know," the other replied.

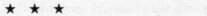

A man had been shipwrecked on a desert island for more than a week when he spotted a boat coming towards him.

"Hurry up, man," said the sailor, "Get on board quickly, there's a tidal wave coming and you'll be drowned."

"No thank you," said the man. "I have faith in Jesus, he will save me."

An hour later, another boat appeared.

"Come on, don't be silly, time's running out, get on board."

"No thanks," said the man again. "I have faith in Jesus, he will save me."

Two hours later, the tidal wave could be seen four miles away. A third boat arrived and the man was urged to get aboard, but he still refused and within half an hour, the island was covered by the tidal wave and the man drowned.

A little later, up in heaven, the man bumped into Jesus.

"I had such faith in you, but you never came to save me and I drowned. I can't believe it," he moaned.

"You can't believe it! What about me?" said Jesus. "I sent three bloody boats to save you!"

There was a knock on the Mother Superior's door.

"Come in," she called.

"Oh Mother Superior, you'll never believe this but we've discovered a case of syphilis," said the nun, visibly shocked.

"Oh good," replied the ageing nun. "I really was getting fed up with the same old muscadet."

Three nuns were talking and one was describing with her hands the huge melons she'd seen at the local market.

The second nun agreed the market was good value and described with her hands the great bananas she's seen.

The third nun, who was very hard of hearing, asked, "Father who?"

Poor old John Gentle. He was such a timid man. Easily upset. One day, he was inside the cathedral courtyard when his stomach suddenly started to rumble and he produced an earth-shattering fart. The whole place went quiet and everyone stared long and hard at him.

Poor, poor John. His embarrassment was more than he could bear. He left town vowing never to return. However, five years went by, John had grown older and now sported a beard. He felt safe enough to return. As he arrived back he walked through the church courtyard once again and was astonished to see that it now had flower beds and a tree-lined avenue.

"I hardly recognise the place," he said to a man passing by. "How long's it been like this?"

"Oh, 18 months and 4 days since John Gentle farted in the courtyard."

One Sunday, the priest happened to notice that one of his congregation took £10 out of the collection, instead of putting something in. He decided to say nothing about it, assuming the poor chap was in dire need of some money.

However the following Sunday it happened again and the priest felt he had to act. After the service was over, he took the man to one side and confronted him with his wrong-doing.

"Oh Father, please forgive me," said the man, blushing profusely.

"I did it because I was in desperate need of a blow job."

Surprised at the reply, the priest made the man promise that he would never steal again. But the incident stayed in the priest's mind and later that evening, he decided to ring his old friend who was Mother Superior at the nearby convent.

"Good evening, Bernadette, sorry to disturb you at such a late hour. I wonder if you could tell me what a blow job is?" She replied immediately. "About £10."

The old farmer was nearing the end of his life and felt the need to confess his sins before it was too late. He went to see the local priest. "Father, I have something to tell you. For over twenty years I've been shagging my goats."

The priest was so stunned, the only thing he could think of saying was "Were they nanny goats or billy goats?"

"Why Father!" said the farmer, deeply shocked, "nanny of course – there's nothing queer about me."

★ ★ ★

EARNING A CRUST

"Hello Mrs Palmer, I'm your husband's boss and I'm just calling to say he'll be late home tonight."
Eager to keep her husband's boss happy, the wife invites him in for a coffee but when he starts to suggest they go upstairs she quickly refuses.
"Come on" says the boss, "I can show you a good time and I'll even give you £300 for the pleasure."
They were short of money so the wife agrees and the deed is done. Later that night, the husband returns home and asks his wife if she has had any visitors.
"Just your boss to tell me you'd be late home" she replies.
"Oh good," he says, "and did he drop off my wage packet?"

A man buys two dogs from the pet shop but after a week he realises he can't keep them apart. They spend all their time humping one another and no matter what he does – throwing cold water over them, putting pepper on their backsides – they carry on regardless. One night, it's so bad the man rings the vet, even though it's 1 o'clock in the morning, and tells him the problem.
"I've got the answer" says the vet, "give each of the dogs a ring on the telephone."
"Really! Will that work?" replies the man, amazed.

151

"Well it bloody well worked for me, you prat!" bellowed the vet as he slammed the phone down.

Two window cleaners were each working on a separate office block when Ted shouted over to his mate,
"Hey Pete, come over here a minute."
Pete put down his sponge and began lowering the cradle to the ground. However, 1m from the bottom, it stuck and as he jumped out, his shirt caught on a nail and ripped the material from top to bottom causing him to lose his balance, fall over and sprain his ankle. He hobbled over to the other building and called the lift so that he could reach his mate who was working on the 20th floor. Unfortunately, the lift was broken, so he had to hobble up the steps, but on the way he slipped on a wet patch and fell into the wall, giving himself a bloody nose. Eventually, he got to the 20th floor and located his mate.
"I'm here Ted, what's up?"
"Cor, you took your time! I just wanted to show you I could see your house from here."

The woman was so pleased with the decorator's work. The house was beautifully fresh and clean. She took her husband upstairs to see the finished results but he'd just been in the garden and left his dirty handprints all over the bedroom

door. She could have cried with disappointment. The next morning when the decorator came to finish off she smiled sweetly at him and said,

"I really can't thank you enough for such a good job. I just wondered if you would mind coming upstairs for a few minutes so that I can show you where my husband put his hand."

The decorator visibly paled and stuttered his reply.

"No thanks, if its all the same to you. Just a letter of recommendation would be nice."

A new colonel had just arrived at the remote outpost. It was his first assignment abroad and he was determined to make a name for himself.

"First of all, I would like a complete tour of the base," he ordered his second in command, and for the next hour the colonel inspected every little nook and cranny, eventually arriving at a small shed.

"What's in there?" he bellowed.

"A camel Sir," came the reply, and it was explained to the colonel that because the outpost was so remote, the men would sometimes get sexually frustrated and then they'd use the camel.

"Disgusting!, get rid of it immediately," he ordered.

Three months went by and the colonel was badly missing the fairer sex. He swallowed his pride and asked if indeed the camel had been removed from camp.

"I'm sorry Sir, it is in fact still here," said the second in command. With that, the colonel went down to the shed, dropped his trousers, got up behind the camel and gave it all he'd got.

"There" he panted, "is that what the men do?"

Thoroughly embarrassed, the second in command replied, "Not exactly, no Sir. The men ride the camel to the nearest whorehouse."

"I would like to be painted in the nude" said the beautiful young girl to the famous artist.

"Okay" replied the artist, "but I'll have to keep my socks on so I have somewhere to put my brushes."

The ticket inspector was checking tickets on the 4.30 to Croydon when she stopped by a man who opened his raincoat and flashed his tackle.

"Oh no, that's no good" she replied with vigour. "I want to see your ticket, not just the stub!"

The man came into work, one arm in a sling, a bandage round his head, 2 black eyes and a painful limp.

"And what time do you call this?" asked his boss. "You're

very late."

"I'm sorry sir, I tripped over the garden step" said the poor man.

"Oh yeah, and it took, a whole hour to do that, did it!" he replied scornfully.

Two men were painting a bridge over the River Seven. One was in a cradle at the top and the other was in a second cradle further down, steadying the ropes.

"Throw me up some paint thinner" shouted the first man.

"Oh thanks" said the second man, who was hard of hearing. "I've been on this diet a month now."

"No, I said throw me up some thinner."

"Yes thanks, I've had my dinner."

"Listen, you stupid prat, I said PAINT THINNER" he bellowed.

"Oh right," and the second man threw him up a bottle of paint thinner which unfortunately hit him on the head causing him to fall out of the cradle and plunge into the icy waters, never to be seen again. The following month, an inquest was held and before the verdict was announced the coroner asked whether anyone present had anything to say. His mate got up and replied,

"Just one thing, Mr Coroner Sir. I think his accident had something to do with sex."

"Really? Why's that?"

"Well, as he passed me going down he shouted 'Cunt'."

★ ★ ★

Two shepherds are driving a lorry full of sheep back to their hillside farm when suddenly the brakes fail as they come hurtling towards a sharp bend in the road.
"Quick," shouted one of the men, "Jump for it!"
"What about the sheep?" shouted the other.
"Oh fuck the sheep," he cried.
"What! do you think we have time?"

★ ★ ★

The electricity man called round at number 63 Ramtop Drive to turn on the power for the new tenants. After knocking at the door for some time it was eventually opened by a small boy.
"Where's your mum, son?" he asked.
The little boy didn't answer but just pointed at the stairs. So, thinking there was something wrong, he went up the stairs and walked into the bedroom. There on the bed was a woman being shagged by a huge billy goat. He rushed back down the stairs, badly shaken by what he had seen, and stammered at the little boy.
"Son, son, do you know what's going on up there, do you know what they're doing?"
The boy just looked at him and then said,
"Na-a-a-a-a."

★ ★ ★

Typists beware!
Johnny also works by touch.
His job was like a pubic hair on a toilet seat.
He was bound to get pissed off eventually.

Secretary to her boss.
"Excuse me Sir, the invisible man's here."
"Well tell him I can't see him," he answered.

His secretary was absolutely useless.
"Why don't you answer the bloody phone?" he said in
exasperation.
"Because I'm damned well fed up," she replied.
"Nine times out of ten it's for you."

Did you hear about the man who lost two fingers working in
the car factory?
Funnily enough he didn't realise he'd lost them until he left
work and waved goodbye to the foreman.

A man was working on the sewage farm when he suddenly lost his footing and slipped in.

"Help, fire, fire, fire!" he yelled.

In no time at all the fire engine responded.

"Where's the fire then?" asked the chief fire officer.

"There isn't one" replied the worker. "But if I'd shouted "shit, shit, shit, no one would have rescued me."

As the man crossed the street he tripped up and broke his watch on the side of the pavement.

"Damn" he muttered, "I must get it mended," and looking around he saw a shop with a huge clock in the window. Thinking it must be a watchmakers, he went in and asked the owner to mend his watch.

"I'm sorry Sir, I don't mend watches, I perform circumcisions."

"Then why do you have a huge clock in your window?" replied the man, feeling somewhat irritated.

"Well what would you put in the window?" said the owner.

A man rings up his boss to tell him he won't be in to work.

"I'm sorry, I'm sick," he tells him.

"Sick again?" says the boss angrily "This seems to be happening a lot. How sick are you?"

"Pretty sick" replies the man. "I'm in bed with my sister."

The multinational company was looking for a new Director General and three men were up for the job. To test their undying loyalty to the company, they were all asked to do the same thing. Go into the other room and shoot your wife," they ordered the first man, handing him a gun.

"Oh no," gasped the man. "My wife means more to me than anything, I can't do it."

So he was dismissed.

The second man was given similar instructions. Handing him a gun they ordered him to go next door and shoot his wife dead.

"I can't do it," replied the ashen-faced man, "Tomorrow is our 25th anniversary and we've lived a very happy life."

So the second man was dismissed.

The third man came in, a gun was passed to him and he was told to go into the next room and kill his wife. The man did as he'd been instructed and went next door. At first there was complete silence but all of a sudden they heard an awful scream, furniture falling over and then all went quiet. A moment later the third man returned.

"What happened in there?" they asked.

"Some prat put blank cartridges in the gun so I had no choice but to strangle her," he replied.

Two simple lads were working in the sawmill when Jack accidentally cut his arm off. As quick as lightening his mate, Pete, put it in a plastic bag and rushed them both to hospital. After four hours the brilliant surgeon had sewn the arm back on and within 3 months Jack was as good as new. That winter Jack was so cold, his concentration slipped and he cut off his right leg. Quick as a flash Pete wrapped up the leg in a plastic bag and rushed them to hospital. Although the operation was more difficult, the surgeon, once again, miraculously attached the leg back to Jack's body and after 6 months he had fully recovered. The months went by until one day Jack fell asleep at work and cut his head off. Ready for every emergency, Pete got the head in a plastic bag and rushed them to hospital.

"This is a very difficult operation" said the surgeon "it's touch and go." He told Pete to come back the following morning to see how things were progressing. The next day Pete arrived at the hospital and met a very serious looking surgeon.

"I'm sorry, your friend didn't make it."

Grief stricken, Pete replied, "I know you did all you could doc, but you did warn me it might not work."

"Oh it wasn't the operation" said the surgeon, "that was successful, but Jack had suffocated in the plastic bag.

The milkman couldn't believe the note left on the doorstep, requesting 60 gallons of milk. Intrigued, he rang the doorbell to make sure the order was correct and a beautiful woman, covered only by a towel opened the door.

"Oh yes" she said, "I read somewhere that bathing in milk did wonders for your sex life."

"Would that be pasteurised?" he asked.

"No, up to my tits is enough," she answered.

A dog walks into a greengrocers carrying a basket and a list in his mouth. He gives the list to the shop assistant and the basket is soon full of apples, oranges, a melon and 2lb plums.

"That'll be £3.50," says the assistant and the dog passes over a purse. He counts out the right money, hands back the purse and the dog leaves the shop. Over the next few weeks the dog appears regularly in the shop and the assistant becomes more and more curious about where he comes from. Eventually he decides that when the dog next comes in, he'll close up and follow the animal home. The following Thursday afternoon the dog appears and the assistant follows him home. It's at least a mile to walk and throughout the journey the dog shows remarkable skills in crossing the many busy roads. At last he walks up the garden path of a squalid looking house and knocks on the door. A moment later it's opened by a fat, scruffy looking man who kicks the dog back down the path. Outraged at such behaviour, the assistant rushes up to the man and shouts:

"How dare you treat this amazing dog in such a callous way?"

"Bugger off," replies the man, "The dog's got to learn. It's the third time this month that he's forgotten his keys."

The man had only been working at the zoo for a week when he was asked to show round a group of foreign tourists. One of the women asked him what the difference was between echidnas and porcupines.

"The echidnas pricks are longer," he replied.

The answer caused great discomfort amongst the group and once they had gone the boss took him to one side and asked him to be more careful with his choice of words in the future.

"It's quills," he said, "use the word quills."

A couple of weeks later another group of tourists were doing the rounds.

"Heh, look at that porcupine," said one of them.

"No Sir," corrected the zoo keeper, "it's an echidna. It's smaller, not so dark and it's quills are longer … but their pricks are about the same size."

It was the local County Show and a new vet was touting for business. He approached an old farmer who was showing off his prize herd of cows.

"Hello Mr Oldham, I'm just setting up a new practice in these parts and I was wondering if you'd ever considered artificial insemination for your cows?"

"No, I haven't," replied the farmer, "and to be honest I don't rightly understand all these modern ways."

"Well, if you change your mind I can always come out to your farm and give you a demonstration" said the vet.

Some weeks went past and the farmer remembered the conversation at the County Show and being curious as to how a cow could be serviced without a bull, he gave the vet a ring.

"OK Mr Oldham," answered the vet, "I'll be out in the morning, just make sure the cow's been washed down, have some clean straw, a bucket of hot water and a stool."

The next day the vet arrived and asked the farmer if all was ready.

"Oh yes," said the farmer, "I've even put a nail on the wall for you to hang up your trousers."

The milk lorry is just leaving the farmyard when it runs over and kills the prize rooster. Upset at what he'd done, the driver seeks out the farmer's wife to tell her what has happened.

"I'm really sorry Madam, I didn't see your rooster until it was too late, but I'd like to replace it."

"Well that's OK with me," she replied. "You'll find the chickens round the back."

A boss called one of his workers into the office.

"Now listen, Simms, you're going to have to pull your socks up or I'll have to sack you. For the past few weeks you've been constantly late, you've made silly mistakes and you've not been civil to your fellow workers. What do you have to say for yourself?"

"I'm sorry, Sir. Things aren't right between me and the wife and I'm sick with worry."

Now the boss was a kindly man, so he gave him some advice. "Now Simms, you've got to show them that you don't take them for granted. Why! Look at me. When I get home I give my wife a long, lingering kiss, give her a present and then make mad passionate love. I'll give you the afternoon off, so why don't you do the same thing?"

"I don't know what to say," gasped Simms. "Thank you very much...by the way, what's your address?"

One of the most important rules in the hand-made chocolate company was that all employees MUST wash their hands after going to the toilet. One day, the boss was passing just as two workers were coming out of the toilet, still zipping their flies up. He stopped them and said angrily, "Did you wash your hands? Remember these are hand-made chocolates."

"No, we don't need to," replied one of them. "It's 12.30 and we're off to lunch!"

A travelling salesman had just delivered to the local farmer when he noticed a horse beckoning him over from a nearby field.

"Look at me in this bloody useless field," said the horse to the man. "I should be treated like royalty, the number of races I've won, everything from the Cheltenham Gold Cup to the Grand National," he boasted.

The salesman looked at the horse in awe. If he owned a talking horse, imagine the money he could make! So he went and sought out the farmer.

"I'd like to buy your horse," he said.

"You don't want him," the farmer replied.

"I certainly do, and I'll give you £50,000 for him," he persisted.

"Okay, it's a deal," said the farmer and they shook hands.

"By the way," asked the man, looking puzzled. "Why wouldn't I want the horse?"

"Because he's a bloody liar, he's never won a race in his life."

A man rings up his ex-boss but is told by the secretary that Mr Grinder has passed away. All day the man continues to ring until the secretary eventually says, "Why do you keep calling?"

"I just like to hear you say it," says the man happily.

165

★ ★ ★

A weary travelling salesman had just spent two weeks visiting all his northern clients but was unable to get home because of bad weather. He was forced to stay at an hotel for the night. Just as he was finishing dinner and preparing to go up to his room, he bumped into one of his best clients who had also been stranded. "I'm so glad to see you, Cooper," said the client, smiling. "Would you mind if I shared your room for the night, the hotel is full?"

Cooper didn't have much choice. Only that day, he'd taken a large order from him so he agreed and they retired to his double-bedded room. However, in the middle of the night, he suddenly felt a hand caress his private parts and a kiss was planted on the side of his face!

Returning home the next day, he told his wife what had happened.

"What did you do?" she asked.

Cooper shrugged his shoulders.

"I didn't have much choice, I couldn't afford to lose such a large order."

The business is doing badly and one of two people from middle management will have to go. It's not an easy decision, as both Theresa and Jack have been there a long time and they're both very good. The first one to leave work tomorrow will get their cards, decides the Personnel

Manager; that's the only way he can think of doing it. The following evening, 30 minutes before she usually leaves, Theresa tells Jack she has a bad headache. It could be a migraine coming on, so she's going to go home early. As she gets her coat, the Personnel Manager spots her and decides to take immediate action. He goes over to her and says, "There's something I have to say to you, Theresa. I'm going to have to lay you or Jack off."

"Jack off!" she retorted angrily. "I've got a bad headache."

FRIENDS AND NEIGHBOURS

Two busybodies were walking through the park slagging everyone off when one says to the other
"Look at her from number 16, breast feeding in public again!"
"Not just that, the boy looks 18 and he's not even her son."

Two neighbours are chatting over the garden wall.
"When my husband comes home from work tonight, he'll probably bring me a huge bunch of flowers."
"Oh isn't that nice, you are lucky."
"No, not really. He'll expect me to take all my clothes off and be on the floor with my legs in the air."
"Oh dear, why's that? Haven't you got any vases?"

Two women talking over the garden fence.
"Why Samantha, you're looking very pleased with yourself, what's been going on?" asked Julie.
"Well I've had the most extraordinary week" replied Samantha.

"Yesterday I answered the door and standing there was a beautiful young man who asked me if Ben was in. When I told him he wasn't, he took me by the hand, led me upstairs, put me on the bed and made love to me all morning. My, he was a big boy! Then yesterday, he came round again, asked if Ben was in and when I said no, he took me back up to the bedroom and had me in 3 different positions for more than 3 hours. He never seems to get tired! Then, would you believe it, he comes back again this morning, asks for Ben and when I tell him Ben is at work, he carries me up to the bedroom and takes me time and time again.

Julie, I can't believe how wonderful it's been. One thing that puzzles me though...why does he want to see Ben?"

"Billy" said the young woman who had moved in next door. "I forgot to get some milk at the corner store, do you think you could go for me?"
"No" said the boy, "but I overheard dad say he could."

Two women talking over the garden fence.
"My husband's an efficiency expert."
"What's that then?"
"Well, I'll put it another way. If a woman did it, they would call it nagging."

"Do you know what mothballs smell like?"

"Yes."

"Goodness. How do you get their little legs apart?"

"What's wrong Rosie, you look a bit glum?"

"It's this new bloke of mine, when we're in bed all he wants to do is 'eat it'."

"Well if you don't want that why don't you try and put him off by rubbing vinegar in your pussy."

A couple of days later they met up again and Rosie's friend asked her "Did it work?"

"No" she moaned, "the night after I'd tried it, he came to bed with a bag of chips."

★ ★ ★

Johnny's neighbour, Mrs Morgan, had a celebrated parrot. People from far and wide would come to see the bird because he was such a wonderful conversationalist. There was only one drawback – the parrot was obsessed with ducks. If he saw a duck he had to shag it and unfortunately for Mrs Morgan there was a farm just across the field and the ducks were forever being rogered by her obsessed parrot. One day the farmer came round in a dreadful rage.

"If ever I see your parrot near my ducks again, I'm going to

170

shoot it dead. My poor ducks are worn out and I won't be having it anymore."

Mrs Morgan turned to her parrot angrily "You hear that, if it happens again I shall punish you so badly you'll never forget it."

A week went by and the parrot behaved himself, but one afternoon when all was quiet he escaped again to do the evil deed.

"That's it!" she screamed, and taking a pair of shears from the garden shed, she cut all the feathers off his head until he was completely bald. The following day, Mrs Morgan was hosting a cocktail party and the parrot was put in the corner and ordered not to move all night. As the guests arrived they were greeted by their hostess and then the parrot in the corner who would say loudly but politely "Good evening Sir, Good evening Madam."

However, the last two guests to enter were both bald and as soon as the parrot caught sight of them he screamed,

"OK, you two duck shaggers, over here in the corner with me."

Three men on the way home from work were moaning about their dull, tedious lives.

"Let's try and liven it up a bit," said one, "I know, when we get home, we'll do exactly whatever our wives tell us to do."

They all shook hands and went their separate ways, agreeing to meet up the next morning and swap stories. The following day, on the way to work the first one told them what happened.

"I got in, lit a cigarette and all of a sudden I sneezed. The cigarette dropped out of my mouth onto our new sofa and burnt a hole.

"Why don't you burn the whole house down while you're at it?" my wife said. "So I did. I haven't seen her since, she stormed off threatening me with divorce."

The second man looked very downcast.

"My wife's gone home to her mother. When I got in last night I decided to mow the lawn but I went over a pebble which flew up and broke the kitchen window and she said, "Well done! Why don't you smash them all?"

"So I did, and that's when she left."

"That's nothing," replied the third man, "My wife's reported me to the police for indecent assault. She'd gone out for the evening and by the time she got home I was already in bed. Of course, when she got in beside me the old todger started to look lively so I put me hand on her pussy but she didn't want to know.

"You can cut that out," she said, "so I did. Does anyone want a toupee?"

What is the definition of a real friend?
One who goes into town and gets two blow jobs, then comes back and gives one to you.

Two women talking over the garden wall. The first said "It's no good Julie, I'm at my wits end. I can't stand the sight of George any longer. He treats me like shit, he's never at home, he just uses the place as an hotel and I know he's shagging everyone in sight. It's had a terrible effect upon me, I've already lost a stone in weight.

"Leave him Sylvia, leave him today and take him for everything you can," replied her outraged friend.

"Oh I will, I will, but first I've just got to lose another half stone."

Finding her cooker had packed in, Beryl called up the repair man and arranged for him to come round on Tuesday morning.

"I won't be in," she said, "but I'll leave my key with the next door neighbour. Please leave the bill with her when you've finished and I'll pop a cheque in the post. Oh, by the way. I've got 'growler' – a very fierce guard dog – but you'll be alright if he sees the neighbour let you in. I've also got a parrot but be warned, whatever you do, please don't say anything to it."

Having been given all the instructions the repair man went round on Tuesday morning and soon had the cooker repaired, although the whole time he'd been there he'd had to put up with a stream of obscenities from the parrot. As he was packing up to go his temper snapped and he turned to the parrot, saying, "You fucking little bastard, drop bloody dead."

The parrot went very quiet and then with a gleam in his eye rose to his full height and said

"Growler, kill...kill growler."

A man looks over his garden wall to see his neighbour digging a hole in the back garden.

"What are you up to?" he asks.

"I'm digging a hole for my dead hamster," he replies.

"Sorry to hear that, but it's a big hole for a hamster isn't it?"

"Of course it is, it's inside your fucking cat" he yells.

Two mates are out fishing for mackerel when their boat hits a rock and sinks almost immediately.

"Help, I can't swim!" cries Jack.

"Don't worry, jump on my back and I'll swim for the shore," replies Colin. For an hour Colin battles with the waves but eventually drags himself up onto the beach.

"Hell fire" he pants "I'm fucked."

"Yes, sorry about that" says Jack "it was the only way I could stay on."

174

"...and another thing" continued the complaining woman, "I now know what eternity feels like. It's the time it takes between you coming and him leaving."

Two men, who've been good friends for years, go off hiking over the Yorkshire Dales. They walk 20 miles during the morning and stop for lunch at the Travellers Rest for sandwiches and a few pints of beer. Of course, halfway through the afternoon Bob is dying for a pee and rushes into the undergrowth to relieve himself. All of a sudden Pete hears a mighty scream and rushing over, he discovers that Bob has been bitten on his todger by a rare snake.

"Don't worry Bob, I'll go and get help," says Pete, and he sets off for the nearest village. The doctor tells him that his mate will die unless he acts immediately.

"You need to suck out all the poison from the wound as soon as possible."

Pete returns to Bob who's lying there in agony.

"What did he say" asks Bob.

"Sorry mate, the doctor says you're going to die."

Three men go away for the weekend on a hunting trip and as they are sitting round the camp fire on the first night, they start bragging.

The first said,

"If it hadn't been for my quick thinking, our next door neighbours would never have survived the fire. I happened to see smoke coming out of an upstairs window, so I immediately rushed into their house and dragged them all from their beds before the whole place went up."

"Very good," said the second man, "but I foiled a daring bank raid. There I was in the bank when these armed men burst through the door and took everyone hostage. With my quick thinking, though, I managed to hide in the utilities cupboard and when all was quiet, I got out and set off the alarm."

The third man said nothing. He just continued stirring the hot ashes with his penis.

Three female friends were walking in the country when they stumbled across a very old bottle, half hidden in the earth. On taking the stopper out, a genie appeared and told them he had the power to grant them more intelligence.

The first woman, who was a 'plain Jane', asked for 50% more intelligence and she was turned into a world renowned surgeon.

The second woman asked for 25% more intelligence and she became a teacher. The third woman who was a bit of a stunner and one for the men, replied

"I don't think I want any. It's good to be dumb, men will do anything for you. In fact, I think I'd like to be even dumber." And on saying that, she turned into a man."

Two old men were gossiping at their old school reunion.

"I hear old Bates is living with a gorilla" said one.

"Well I never, is it male or female?"

"Female of course. You know old Bates, there's nothing unnatural about him."

Two young girls talking over the garden fence.

"Honestly Fiona, my new boyfriend's got submarine hands."

"What do you mean?"

"You never know where they'll turn up next."

A very poor, uneducated and plain woman found herself in dire straits. She was only 30 but already she had 5 children and her husband had abandoned her. A kindly welfare worker took the family on and managed to re-house them, sort out debts and get her a little job. A year went by before the welfare worker saw the woman again, but to her shock and amazement she was 5 months pregnant.

"Oh no, why have you done this, you were just getting back on your feet and building up your self respect. Whose is it?"

The woman looked tearful and replied,

"It's the next door neighbours. I was just so flattered that he'd actually asked me."

Sitting over his pint of beer, the man looked very downcast. "What's wrong?" asked the bartender.

"I tell you what's wrong" he said, "nobody appreciates me round here. Look what I did for the old people's home, putting on that musical evening to raise money for their outing. But do they call me Fred the entertainer? No. Then look what I did with that piece of wasteland. Changed it into a park for everyone to enjoy. But did they call me Fred the landscape artist? Not bloody likely. Yet, he said, sadly taking another sip of beer, "just one, just one bloody sheep..."

Two women are talking over the garden wall and one is complaining about her piles.

The other says to her,

"I know just the remedy. Stick some tea leaves up there and you'll soon be cured."

However, this remedy doesn't work so the woman is forced to go to the doctors.

"Bend over please," he says, and while he's examining her she asks him if he can see anything.

"Not a lot," replies the doctor, "but I can forecast that you're going to come into some money and spend it on a round the world cruise."

A single man moved in next door to a couple and it wasn't long before he and the wife became attracted to each other, but they managed to keep their feelings in check. Then one hot summer's afternoon, the single man went round for afternoon tea. While there, he noticed the couple's guttering was full of weeds so he volunteered to go up the ladder and clear it for them. While he was up there, the couple lay out on the lawn sunbathing and as the husband rubbed sun lotion on his wife's back, the man shouted down.

"Heh, you two, no sex down there!"

"We're not!" they yelled.

A couple of minutes went by and the man up the ladder shouted again.

"Hey, stop all that sex!"

Again, they shouted up, "We're not having sex."

Some time later, the man came down for a rest and the husband said he'd finish off. So up he went leaving his wife and next door neighbour sunbathing on the lawn. The nearness of their bodies was too much for them and soon they were making mad passionate love.

"Well, bugger me," said the husband, looking down from the ladder. "Up here, it really does look as if they're having sex."

A couple and their precocious son moved into the close and invited all their neighbours round for a 'getting to know you' cocktail party. Unfortunately, the young son, who should have been in bed, kept coming back down and bothering his parents. "Don't worry," said the retired Sergeant-Major, "I'll soon get the boy settled."

After a few minutes the guest rejoined the party and nothing more was seen of the son. The party was a great success and everyone left a little the worse for wear.

"Oh, by the way," said the couple to the Sergeant-Major as he was putting on his coat to leave, "Thank you for settling down our son, what is your secret?"

"Oh quite simple really, I just taught him how to masturbate."

Three women were discussing safe sex. The first said she used the pill, the second said she always carried a packet of condoms and the third said she always used a tin with a few pebbles inside. The other two looked at her in amazement.

"How does that work?" they asked.

"Oh, it's easy really. I get the man to stand on the tin and when I hear the pebbles start to rattle I kick it out from under him."

Two women are talking over the garden wall and the conversation turns to money.

"You know, Lauren, I've discovered a great way to get more money out of my old man. Last week I wore a low necked jumper when we went shopping and as I bent over the supermarket freezer one of my boobs popped out. You should have seen Bill, he nearly had a blue fit. I told him it was because I didn't have enough money to buy a new bra so he's increased my housekeeping. You ought to try it."

The following week, the two women met up for another chat and Lauren was asked if she had taken her friend's advice.

"Oh, it was a disaster," exclaimed Lauren. "We were just about to go down the bingo when I lifted my skirt and told my husband I had no knickers on because I couldn't afford to buy any. The old skinflint, he threw me a quid and told me to buy a comb. At least you can look tidy, he said."

Two women were talking over the garden wall.

"Well come on Stace, how did your new hot date go last night?"

"Okay, I suppose, but I don't think I'll be going out with him again."

"Why not?"

"Well, he's a French Horn player and everytime we kissed, he stuck his fist up my backside!"

Two men were returning from a sales conference. One turned to the other and said

"When I get home, I'm going to pour myself a large gin and tonic and put my feet up. What about you, Bob?"

"I'm going to tear my wife's knickers off," replied Bob.
"Gosh! I didn't know you and your wife were still so passionate!"
"We're not. It's just that her knickers are far too tight round my waist."

Two fishing pals meet up on the riverbank.
"Hello, Bob," says his mate. "Long time no see, what've you been up to?"
Bob shakes his head sadly.
"I've been on my honeymoon."
"Well, you sly old fox! You kept that quiet. I bet she's a pretty lass."
"No, not at all. In fact she's ugly...and she's useless in bed," Bob replies mournfully.
"But, I don't understand. Why did you marry her then?"
"She's got worms."

Two young whales, one male, one female, grew up together happily roaming the ocean and enjoying each other's company. But one day the peace was shattered when one of the whales spotted a trawler.
"That's the bastard that killed my mum. Come on! I want to get my own back, will you help me?" he said.
"What are you going to do?" asked the other.

"I have an idea that if we both swim underneath the boat and spurt out water from our blow holes, we'll manage to capsize the boat."

So they carried out the plan and it worked perfectly. The trawler capsized and some of the survivors were left floundering in the water.

"Heh! We can't let them get away," said the avenging whale, "Will you help me to eat them up?"

"Now hold on a minute," she replied. "I didn't mind helping you with the blow job but there's no way I'm going to swallow any seamen."

Three women met up for tea and couldn't help but boast about their husbands. "Well of course, my husband is now a high court judge. It was expected. He's had a brilliant career," said the first.

"My Gerald runs the Foreign Office," said the second.

"Now my husband, Martell…"

"Wait a minute," interrupted the first lady, "isn't Martell a liquor?"

The third lady was amazed. "How did you know, have you met him?"

Two young women talking over the garden wall. "You know Julie, this is the last straw," said Carry. "I've had it up to here

183

with men, they lie, cheat and are no damned good. From now on, if I want sex, I'll use a vibrator."

"But what if the batteries run out, what will you do then?" she asked her friend.

"Then I'll do what I did with Harry, I'll fake an orgasm."

Three sisters, named **Flora, Fiona** and **Fanny** lived in the same village in Yorkshire and were renowned for their beauty, although all of them had extra large feet. One evening, Flora and Fiona went to the local village bop and were soon chatting to some lads from the next village.

"By gum," said one of the lads. "Haven't you got big feet!"

"Oh that's nought" they replied. "You should see our Fanny's."

PLAYTIME

The parachutist was distraught to find his parachute had failed to open and he was hurtling towards the ground at a fantastic rate. He was sure he was about to meet a sticky end. Suddenly, as he looked down he saw a group of men standing in a circle. They were shouting, "We'll catch you, don't worry, we'll catch you."

The relief the man felt was unbelievable, until he looked again at the group and realised they were the English cricket team.

Three farmers are walking across the mountainside when they spot a field of sheep.
"Heh, there's some good looking sheep over there," the first one jokes. I wish one was Jordan."
"I wish one was Baby Spice," says the second.
"I wish it was dark," whispers the third.

Two men are changing in the dressing rooms after playing a game of badminton. After showering, one of them puts on bra and pants.

"Heh, what's going on here?" asks his mate, how long have

you been wearing these?"
"Ever since my wife found them in my car," he replies.

A man went along to a 'spooks' evening at the local Town Hall to hear guest speakers talk about their strange experiences. Sitting at the back, he couldn't hear all that was being said and he began to doze off when suddenly one of the speakers asked loudly,
"Now come on, don't be shy, there must be someone here whose had a relationship with a ghost?"
Without thinking, the man put his hand up and was asked to come down to the front.
"Ladies and Gentlemen, this gentlemen here has kindly volunteered to tell us about his intimate relationship with a ghost. Please give him a warm hand."
But the man had come to a sudden halt.
"Ghost!" he exclaimed. "I thought you said goats."

A kindly middle-aged woman was walking through the shopping arcade when she saw a scruffy man sitting on one of the benches. Overcome with pity, she went up to him and put £5 in his hand.
"Here you are, young man, have faith do you hear, have faith."
A week later, she was walking through the arcade again when the same scruffy man ran up to her.

"I've been looking for you," he said.

"Have Faith came in at 16/1, here's your winnings" and he put a wad of notes in her hand.

A man went into the bookies and left his big Alsatian outside tied to a post. Some minutes later, another man came rushing in looking very distraught. He said to the man
"Is that your dog outside?"
"Yes" he replied.
"Oh, bloody hell, I think my dog's killed him."
"What!" roared the man "What kind of dog have you got?"
"A peke."
"A peke! but how could a small dog like that kill my dog?" said the puzzled man.
"I think it got stuck in his throat" came the reply.

A Scotsman, on the way home from a heavy drinking session with his mates, collapses onto a park bench and falls into a very deep stupor. Some time later 2 girls walk past and on seeing him debate whether he has anything under his kilt. They decide to look and discover he's stark naked.

"We really ought to leave him a record of our visit," one says to the other, so giggling with delight they tie a blue ribbon round his willy before moving on. Finally the Scotsman comes round and staggers behind a bush bursting for a pee.

When he sees the ribbon he smiles and says to it
"I don't know where or what you've been up to, but I see you've won first prize!"

The man sat at the bar looking morosely into his pint of beer. No matter how hard he tried to ignore it, a little voice inside his head kept on and on at him
"How could you Bob, how could you sleep with one of your patients!"
Time went by, and a few more pints disappeared down his throat until he began to feel a little better – even the voice inside his head began to mellow.
"OK Bob, I suppose you're not the first person to sleep with one of their patients and no matter what they say, you're still the best vet in the district."

★ ★ ★

A man walks into a wine bar, sits down at a table and studies the menu. A couple of minutes later he looks up to see a beautiful waitress standing in front of him. She is so gorgeous that he gasps with pure lust.
"What would you like?" she asks.
"A glass of claret and a quickie please," he replies, drooling at the mouth. The waitress is so disgusted she storms off but returns a few minutes later when she has calmed down. Again she asks "What would you like?"

He smiles and says again, "A glass of claret and a quickie please."

"That's it" she yells, gives him a sharp slap across the face and stomps off.

The man sits there dumbstruck when suddenly from the next table a fellow customer leans over and whispers "I think it's pronounced 'quiche'."

Johnny was looking for his mate Bob Cox and thought he might be having his hair cut. He popped his head round the barber shop door and called out, "Bob Cox in here?"

"Sorry, no" replied the barber, "We only do shaves and haircuts."

Did you hear about the beautiful blonde hitchhiker?

A passing motorist picked her up and asked her what she did for a living.

"I'm a magician," she said.

"Never! Go on prove it" he replied.

So she touched him on his leg and turned him into an hotel.

An old vicar was retiring and selling his horse so he put an ad in the local newspaper. It wasn't long before it was bought by

Bob who decided to ride it home. But when he mounted up, the horse wouldn't move.

"I trained this horse from a little foal," said the vicar.

"He only moves when you say 'Jesus Christ' and stops when you say 'Amen'."

Bob thanked the vicar and sure enough when he said 'Jesus Christ', the horse set off.

On the way home they were caught in a ferocious thunderstorm and the horse bolted when there was a particularly loud crack of thunder. By the time Bob had recovered his wits, the horse was galloping madly through the countryside and it took him a moment or two to remember to say 'Amen'. Immediately the horse came to a standstill, teetering right on the edge of a deep canyon. "Jesus Christ!" he said.

A man walked into the barbers shop and said he wanted his hair to be styled completely different to everyone else.

"Can you part my hair from ear to ear?" he asked.

"If that's what you want," replied the barber doubtfully, and the man was given what he wanted.

However, that afternoon he walked back into the shop.

"What's wrong?" asked the barber. "Are you tired of the style already?"

"No," he replied angrily, "I'm just fed up with everybody whispering in my nose."

Jack, from the neighbouring farm, happened to see his mate
Bill gathering in the harvest without any trousers on.
"Hey Bill, how come you're out here with no trousers on?"
"Well Jack, it's like this. Last week in that hot sun I was out
all afternoon without a shirt on. Bloody hell, I suffered the
next day. My neck was as stiff as a plank...so this is my wife's
idea."

Did you hear what happened when there was a blackout in
London last week?
The musical *Oh! Calcutta!* was temporarily renamed "*Fanny by
gaslight.*"

A nymphomaniac was doing her gardening one Sunday
afternoon when the wind blew her skirt up to reveal a bare
backside. At this moment a dog appeared in the garden and
stuck his tongue in her crotch. Without looking around she
whispered,
"Whoever you are, I do the gardening three times a week,
Sunday afternoon, Friday and Saturday mornings."

"What on earth is that?" said the woman to the waiter.

"It's pressed tongue, Madam."

"Good gracious! I could never eat anything that came out of an animal's mouth. Bring me a boiled egg, please."

A young, rich lawyer had a very bad car crash. The Porsche was a write-off but even worse, the lawyer's arm had been severed. When the paramedics arrived, they heard him whimpering,

"My car, oh my poor car."

"Sir," said one of the helpers, "I think you should be more concerned about your arm."

The lawyer looked round and seeing just his shoulder, exclaimed,

"Oh no, my Rolex, my Rolex."

A pompous upper class prat went duck hunting but no matter how hard he tried, it was more than 6 hours before he managed to shoot one down. Delighted at his sudden luck, he searched for the fallen duck and found it in a nearby field. As he was about to pick it up, a farmer appeared and said aggressively

"What the hell do you think you're doing?"

"I'm getting my duck," he replied.

"Oh no you ain't. This here's my property so it's mine."

"But I've spent all day trying to get a duck and you're not taking it away from me" he spluttered.

And so they argued on, until the farmer came up with a solution:

"Look here, there's one way we could settle this argument. We'll take it in turns to kick each other in the balls and the last man on his feet gets the duck."

The hunter agreed, and the farmer went first because, as he said, it was his idea. Wearing steel capped, hob nailed boots he aimed carefully at the hunter and gave an almighty kick. His poor victim turned a sickly white, his eyes disappeared and he gave out the most agonising cry. It took at least 5 minutes for him to come to his senses but he bravely stayed on his feet.

"Right" he gasped "Now it's my turn."

The farmer replied,

"Don't bother, you can have the duck."

"Hey George, I had a great dream last night. I dreamt I was in a boat with Bo Derek."

"Really! How did it go?"

"Oh it was great, we caught a 10 lb salmon."

193

FOOTBALL

Two Manchester United fans are walking along the street when one of them sees a mirror on the ground. He picks it up and says, "Hey, I recognise that bloke."
The other man takes it from him and replies,
"Of course you do, you wanker, it's me."

Which 3 league teams have swear words in their names?
Arsenal, Scunthorpe United and fucking Chelsea.

A Torquay United fan is walking through the park one day when he stumbles over an old lamp. A genie pops out and tells him he has just one wish, what would he like? The man looks down at his dog and tells the genie he would like his dog to win the Crufts Dog Show to become supreme champion.
"You've got to be joking," replies the genie, "Just look at him. He must be on his last legs, he's a flea bitten old mongrel with half a tail."
"OK," sighs the man, "in that case can you make Torquay win the FA Cup?"
The genie looks at him for a moment and then says, "OK, let's have another look at the dog then."

A footballer got kicked in his vital parts and lay doubled up on the ground holding himself and moaning.

"Are you alright mate?" asked the first-aid man, rushing up to him.

"For Christ's sake," groaned the man. "Whatever you do, don't rub them, just count them!"

Every weekend, her husband would be out playing football with his local team and while he was away, Gloria would entertain her lover. However, disaster struck one afternoon when the pitch was so waterlogged that the husband came back early.

"Quick," whispered the wife, "crouch down behind the sofa, it's too late to get away."

Unfortunately, the husband settled himself down and didn't look as if he was going to move.

"Bugger this," muttered the lover to himself, and he stood up wearing only jockey shorts and a vest saying, as he walked out of the door, "Bloody weather, can't see a thing, you didn't see which way the cross country runners went?"

Visiting a strange town for the night, Roger decided to go and see their local football team who were playing in a cup match. As he arrived, he saw the team posing on the pitch and one man holding the ball on his shoulder.

"What's going on?" he asked the man next to him.

"It won't be long, they're just posing for this week's 'Spot the Ball' competition," he replied.

The manager was talking to his new midfield player.

"We've got a much more important match on Saturday so tonight you'll just play the first half and I'll pull you off at half time."

"Gee Boss, thanks. At half time at my old club, all we got was a slice of orange."

The manager came into the dressing room as the team were changing for the match.

"Where's Bob?" he demanded.

"He sends his apologies, Boss, but he's getting married at 2.45."

"Bloody hell, that means he won't be here to play until the second half."

Three aged football fanatics visit a spiritualist to find out what the future has in store for their teams. When God has

196

been contacted, the first one asks, "When will Manchester United win the European Cup?"

"Within the next ten years," replies God.

"Oh bugger, I'll probably be dead by then."

So the second old man asks God, "When will Torquay United win promotion to the Premier Division?"

"In the next fifty years," comes the reply.

"Hell fire, I'll definitely be dead by then."

Finally, the third man asks, "When will England win the World Cup?"

"You must be joking," says God. "I'll be dead by then."

GOLF

"Darling," said his wife, "if I died before you, do you think you would get married again?"

"Maybe," he replied.

"And would you do all the little things we did together."

"Maybe."

"Would you give her my special golf clubs?"

"Oh no, she's right handed."

And what about the world's worst golfer?
He stood on a rake and bellowed
"That's the best two balls I've hit today."

It was love at first sight. After knowing each other for less than a month, they decide to get married.

"I think I ought to tell you," said the man, "that I'm absolutely golf mad and I like to spend all weekend on the greens."

"Okay" she replied "but there's something I ought to tell you. I'm a hooker."

"Not to worry. We'll soon put that right, it's probably the way you hold the club," he said.

Another couple had a whirlwind romance and were married less than six months after they met. On their honeymoon night, she confessed to him that one of her previous lovers had been his old golfing partner.

"Let's not bring up the past," he said, "all that matters now is that we're together."

For the next hour, they made mad passionate love and when they finally finished he picked up the phone.

"What are you doing?" she asked.

"All that exercise, has made me hungry" he replied. "I'm going to order some steaks and a bottle of bubbly – it is our wedding night after all."

"Oh, but your ex golfing partner would have made love to me again."

Not to be thought second best, the new husband began again and gave it all his worth for the next 45 minutes, after which he laid back on the bed totally exhausted. Again, he tried to ring room service but again she asked for more. At the end of another 30 minutes, he picked up the phone before his wife could speak, saying dejectedly. "Don't worry, it's not room service, I'm just ringing my ex golfing partner to find out what the par for the hole is."

"What's up Bill? You look miserable."
"The doctor's told me I should give up golf."

"Mmm, he's seen you play too, has he?"

Three blokes met up to play golf on Sunday morning and compared notes on how they managed to get their wives to let them go. The first said he'd brought his wife breakfast in bed, taken the dog for an early morning walk and washed the car. "She was so pleased, she was delighted to let me go," he said. The second man recounted how he'd prepared everything for Sunday lunch and cleared up the kitchen from a dinner party the night before.
"She reckoned I'd earned a round of golf," he said.
The third man looked at his mates and said
"I woke up, belched twice, scratched my balls and let rip with a real stinker. Then I said to her, "Come on then, intercourse or golf course? She couldn't wait to see me go."

Jack and his wife were playing a round of golf but on the seventh tee, Jack's ball landed behind the maintenance shed. "Don't worry," said his wife, "there's no need to take a penalty shot, if we open both doors and take out the mowers you can drive straight through."
They did as she suggested and he gave the ball a mighty hit. Unfortunately he missed the far opening and the ball ricocheted back and hit his wife in the head, killing her instantly.

200

A couple of days later he was playing a round of golf with his friend and to his astonishment, ended up in a similar position.

"No need to take a penalty shot" said his friend, "Just open the doors at either end of the shed and hit the ball through."

"Not bloody likely," replied the man. "I tried that a couple of days ago and ended up with a double bogey."

An irritable old man was taking a short cut across the golf course when he got struck by a golf ball.

"I'm terribly sorry," said the player, running up to him.

"That's not good enough. I've got a weak heart, anything could have happened. I demand £500 in compensation."

"But I said fore," exclaimed the player.

"OK, done," replied the man.

"I really want to give this my best shot" said Jack to his mate. "My mother-in-law is watching from the clubhouse balcony."

"Oh get away!" replied his friend. "It's too far away, you couldn't possibly hit her from here."

A man drives his Rolls Royce into the golf club car park and as he's getting his clubs out of the boot a fellow member comes up to him.

"That really is a beautiful car" he says. "May I ask how much it cost you?"

"Oh about £250,000," replies the man, looking pleased.

"And how long have you had it?" he continues.

"About 4 years, I work for Cunard you know."

"So what!" retorted the man "I work fuckin' hard too, but I still couldn't afford a Rolls Royce."

The pompous club pro was challenged to a round of golf by one of the less experienced members for a prize of £100. The pro, smiling to himself, immediately took up the challenge, "but," said his partner, "as long as you agree that I can have two 'geronimos'." Not knowing what these were, but confident in his own ability, the club pro agrees. At the end of the round, the other members are astonished to see the pro handing over £100.

"We can't believe it" they said. "What happened?"

"Well, I was just swinging my club down for the first hole, when my partner grabs me by the bollocks and shouts 'geronimo'." Imagine trying to play the next 17 holes, waiting for the second one."

Dee had been moaning at Pete for ages because he wouldn't teach her golf. Eventually it got him down so much he gave in and took her out one Monday afternoon. After spending some time explaining the finer points of the game they stepped up to the 1st tee and Dee hit a mighty drive which landed straight onto the green and disappeared into the hole. "OK," said Pete, "I'll take a practice shot now, and then we'll begin."

A man has been stranded on a desert island for eight years and then one day he sees a beautiful girl sail ashore in a small boat. She comes over to him and is amazed to learn how long he has been forced to live alone.
"Would you like a drink?" she asks.
"Oh yes please."
And she gets a crate of whisky from the boat.
"Do you smoke?"
"I do."
And she hands him a packet of cigarettes.
After a few minutes she looks at him closely and says, "Now, would you like to play around?"
"Oh my goodness," he gasps, absolutely amazed. "I can't believe you have a set of golf clubs on board as well."

The men were talking in the clubhouse bar after spending a day on the greens. Each was recounting their golfing experiences.

One said, "If I'm going round on my own, the dog comes to keep me company and if I go one over par on a hole he somersaults backwards.

"That's incredible!" responded the others.

Warming to the subject, the man continued.

"Yes, and if I go 2 over par at a hole, he does a double somersault backwards."

"Amazing," came the response, "that's quite a feat, how does he do it."

"Oh I kick him twice."

Two lady golfers were teeing off on the 7th hole when the second player's shot went so wide it hit a man on the 8th tee. He clasped his hands to his crotch in agony as he fell to the ground.

"Oh I'm so very sorry," said the woman as she ran over to help him. "Is there anything I can do? I'm a masseuse so I might be able to ease the pain."

With that, she ordered the man to lay out on the ground, put his hands by his side, undid his trousers and started to massage his manhood. "There, is that helping?" she asked looking very concerned.

"That's great," he replied, "but my finger is still throbbing."

"What's wrong, Fiona?" asked Samantha, seeing her friend in floods of tears.

"It's Dan, he's left me."

"Oh get away, he's always walking out on you."

"No, no, you don't understand. This time it's for good, he's taken his golf clubs."

A golfer teed off on the 10th hole but the ball disappeared over some trees and was never to be seen again. Some time later, he saw a policeman coming towards him on the 12th hole.

"When you were on the 10th, did your ball disappear over that clump of trees?" asked the policeman.

"Yes, it did. Why?" said the puzzled golfer.

"On the other side of those trees is a road. The ball bounced in front of a car causing it to swerve and run over a cat. It then smashed through a window of the house opposite, shocking a man into a fatal heart attack and frightening his wife into dropping her tea and badly burning her leg."

"Bloody hell," said the golfer, who had deathly pale.

"Is there anything I can do?"

"Yes, I think so," replied the policeman. "In future, before you tee off, stand with your legs a little further apart and keep your head still when you swing the club."

PARTY ANIMAL

At the breakfast table the next morning the husband put his head in his hands and groaned loudly.

"Oh bloody hell, what a party last night, I can't remember a thing about it. Did I make a prat of myself?"

"You sure did," replied his wife. "You put your hand up the skirt of your boss's wife and told your boss to piss off."

"Shit! What happened?"

"He sacked you."

"Well, fuck him, the bastard."

"I did," replied the wife, "and you've got your job back."

A man arrived at a party half-way through the evening to find most of the guests in the middle of a frenzied party game.

"What's going on here?" he asked.

"Oh come and join in," he was urged. "It's a great game. All the girls are blindfolded and they have to go round guessing who the men are by feeling their private bits."

The man hesitated.

"Oh I'm not sure about that," he said.

"Don't be daft," came the reply. "Your name's been called out four times already!"

After a wild party the night before, both husband and wife woke up with dreadful hangovers.

"Last night in the garden, was it you I made love to?" asked the befuddled husband.

"I don't know," replied the wife. "You wouldn't happen to know what time that was?"

PUBBING

Two men were sitting at the bar talking over past times. One said to the other, "I'll never forget the day I turned to the bottle as a substitute for women."

"Why's that then?" replied the other.

"I got my dick stuck in it."

Two naive young men were sitting in the park talking.

"Tell you what, Jake," said Maurice. "Let's go down the new pub tonight, 'The Crown and Sceptre'. I've heard it's right good. After you've bought the first drink, the rest are free for the whole night. And then," he grinned conspirationally, "you goes out the back and has sex."

"Are you sure?" asked Jake doubtfully.

"Oh yeah, it was my sister wot told me. That's wot happened to her when she went down there the other night."

A man came staggering through the park, well and truly pissed when he saw another man doing press-ups. After watching him for a minute or two, the drunk started to laugh.

"What's so funny?" asked the man angrily.

208

"I think you ought to know that someone's stolen your woman," he replied.

A man had a very clever parrot whose memory was second to none. One day, the man came up with a foolproof way of making lots of money. He got the parrot to learn the National Anthem and then took it down the pub where he told the customers, "I bet £10 that my parrot can sing the whole of the National Anthem."
Some interest was shown and the money was placed on the bar. Sadly though, the parrot never uttered a note and the man had to pay out a lot of money. When he got home, he was beside himself with rage.
"You bloody stupid, half-witted bird. You've lost me a lot of money today."
"Now wait up a minute," said the clever old bird. "Just imagine the interest you'll get tomorrow when we go back."

A local man walks into the pub knowing that the man behind the bar is short of money after spending all his wages on the horses.
"Hello Pete, fancy a bet?" says the man. "I bet you £100 that I can piss into this empty beer glass."
The bartender agrees, so the man drops his trousers and pisses everywhere – on the floor, the bar, the tables, even on

the bartender himself. The bartender smiles and demands his money.

"OK, Pete, won't be a moment," says the man and he walks over to three men at the other end of the room and comes back with £300 in his hand.

"Here you are, bartender", and he hands over the £100.

"Just a moment," says Pete, looking puzzled. "What's going on over there?"

The man smiles.

"Well, earlier today I made a bet with those three men that I could piss all over your pub and you'd still be smiling at the end of it."

A man walks into a bar with a ferret on his shoulder.

"Sorry, Sir, no ferrets in here," says the landlord. "You'll have to go elsewhere."

"Now hold on a minute," says the man, "this ferret does the best blow job ever."

"Get out of here," bellows the landlord angrily. "I don't have to listen to such crap."

"No really," persists the man. "If you don't believe me, take him out the back and see for yourself."

So the landlord goes out the back and reappears some time later with a big smile on his face.

"That was bloody fantastic," he says. "How much do you want for him?"

"Oh, he's not for sale."

But the landlord insists and after a certain amount of bargaining, they agree on a price of £1,200. When the bar has closed, the landlord takes the ferret home and finds his wife in the kitchen.

"Gloria! teach this ferret how to keep house, then pack your bags and bugger off."

A man walks into a pub and orders a pint of beer and a pasty.

"How much will that be?" he asks.

"Nothing, Sir, it's on the house."

A little later, he orders another beer and again is told it's on the house. After a third pint, he questions the barman.

"Why are all the drinks free today?"

"Oh, it's quite simple really, Sir," replies the barman. "The owner of this pub doesn't know that I know he's upstairs with my wife. So I'm doing to him down here, what he's doing to me up there."

A fire engine came racing around the corner and disappeared up the road, bells clanging wildly. As it passed The Flying Horse, a drunk staggered out and started chasing it, but after a minute or so he collapsed on the ground breathing heavily.

"Bugger it," he gasped. "You can keep your bloody ice creams."

"Oh Bob," sighed his wife. "I wish you wouldn't go down the pub every night. You drink far too much. Here, let me show you something."

Bob's wife put two glasses before him, one filled with whisky, the other with water. Into each she dropped a worm. The worm in the water swam around happily while the worm in the whisky had a fit and sank to the bottom, dead.

"There!" said the wife triumphantly. "Now what does that show you?"

Bob looked at the two glasses and replied, "It shows me that if you drink, you won't get worms. Now I'm off to the pub."

"I'm sorry, Sir, you can't bring that dog into the pub, it's against the rules," said the barman.

"Aah, but this isn't just any dog, this is special. He'll do anything you ask him," boasted the customer.

"OK, tell him to go and get me a newspaper."

The man gave the dog £5 and off he ran. Time went by and the dog didn't return. After an hour, the owner decided to go and look for it. He roamed the streets for ages, until eventually he found the dog in a dark alley humping a bitch.

"What's all this about, you've never let me down before?" complained the man.

"Maybe," replied the dog, "but I've never had so much money before."

A man walked up to the bar and asked for a pint of less.
"Less?" questioned the barmaid, "I've never heard of it, is it a new beer?"
"I don't know," replied the man. "When I went to the doctor's this morning, he told me I should drink less."

A group of men standing at the bar were watching a bloke sitting in the far corner, surrounded by gorgeous women.
"I can't understand it," said one of the onlookers. "What's he got that the rest of us haven't?"
The others shook their heads dejectedly.
"I don't know," said the barman. "Every day he comes in, he doesn't have much money, he dresses conservatively, and all he does is sit there licking his eyebrows."

A man walks into a bar followed by an alligator. He gets everybody's attention and then hits the alligator over the head with an empty beer bottle. Ouch! The stunned beast slowly opens his mouth, the man undoes his trousers and puts his dick inside its mouth. He pulls it out just in time before the alligator's mouth snaps shut.
"Now, ladies and gentlemen," he announces to a stunned audience. "I dare anyone to do the same for a bet of £100."

213

There is a hushed silence and then suddenly an old woman's voice is heard.

"OK, I'll take on the bet, but just don't hit me too hard with the bottle."

"Whisky on the rocks, bartender, please," says the man, and as he gulps it down in one go he takes out a picture from his back pocket.

"Another whisky, please," and again he gulps it down and looks at the picture in his back pocket. For the next 2 hours he goes through the same routine, time and time again. By the end of the night he turns to stagger out when the bartender taps him on the shoulder.

"Sorry, mate, but I have to ask," said the bartender. "You've ordered whiskies all night and each time you've drunk one, you've taken out a picture in your back pocket and looked at it. May I ask why?"

"Sure," replied the man, sounding very pissed. "It's a picture of my wife and when I think she's looking good, then it's time for me to go home."

A sailor had been away at sea for six months so as soon as he landed back on shore he headed for the nearest waterfront bar. Inside the 'Paradiso' a few men were standing at the bar, a pianist was tinkling on the ivories in the corner and a monkey was hanging from the rafters. The sailor went up to the bar and asked for a beer but before he could take a gulp the monkey swung down and pissed in the glass.

"What!" roared the sailor. "Did you see that? Get me another drink."

A second pint of beer was put before him and again the monkey swung down and weed all over it.

The sailor was incensed and grabbed the barman by his shirt front, threatening him with all manner of punishment.

"Hold on, mate," said the barman, "it's not my monkey, it's the pianist's over there. The sailor marched over to the corner and confronted the piano player.

"Do you know your monkey's pissing in my beer?" he roared. The pianist thought for a moment and then replied, "No, but if you hum the tune, I'll soon pick up the melody."

Two mates were talking over a pint of beer.

"What's wrong, Jack, you don't look so good," said Bob.

"It's this bloody toothache, been driving me mad, I just can't get rid of it."

"Well, maybe I can help you there. I had a toothache a couple of months ago and believe it or not my wife gave me a blow job and I was cured. Why don't you try it?"

"Thanks, Jack, I'll have a go. Will your wife be home tonight?"

The bar was empty except for two men and very soon they got talking and commenting about "life".

"Let me tell you something, you can find out a lot about a person very quickly if you know the right question to ask," said the pompous one.

"Is that so?" replied the dimwitted man. "Tell me more."

"Well, say for example that I ask you if you have a dog."

"I do," he replied.

"Well, in that case I assume you have a backyard to keep it in."

"I do," he replied.

"Then I also assume you have a house to go with the backyard."

"I do, I do," he replied, quite amazed.

"And if you have a house, I think you're probably married."

"I am."

"So I assume you're not gay."

"No, I'm not."

"So there you are," said the pompous man. "Just by asking you whether you have a dog I'm able to deduce that you are married, not gay, and live in a house."

"That's astounding," replied the other, "truly astounding."

A couple of weeks went by and one Thursday lunchtime the dimwitted man found himself back in the same bar. Again it was very quiet apart from a stranger sitting close by.

"Excuse me," said the man who had been eager to put his newly acquired knowledge to the test. "May I ask you whether you have a dog?"

"No I don't," replied the stranger. At that, the man quickly

216

pushed back his chair and headed for the door saying as he went, "Then I'm not stopping round here with a bloody poof."

A man walks into a pub, orders a pint of beer and asks the barman if he can borrow the pub's newspaper and do the crossword.

The barman thinks for a moment and then replies, "I'd just like to ask you a couple of questions first. Tell me, when a sheep dumps why does it come out in little dottles?"

The man shook his head. "I don't know."

"OK," said the barman. "What about cows, why does it come out in a round 'pat'?"

Again the man shook his head.

"Listen, mate," said the barman scornfully. "You don't know shit, so I don't reckon you'll be able to do the crossword!"

A man walks into a pub and the locals ask him if he would like to play bar football.

"Yes," replies the man, "but what do I have to do?"

"Oh it's quite easy – drink beer, piss and then fart."

So the man does as he has been told. Then one of the locals tells him, "If you can do it again, you'll get an extra point."

So the man obliges. He drinks the beer, pulls down his trousers to take a piss but before he has time to fart one of the locals shoves his finger up the man's arse.

"Heh! What the hell's going on?" asks the man.

"Just blocking the point," comes the reply.

A man walks into a bar with a Cornish pasty on his head and asks the barman for a pint of beer. Unable to conceal his curiosity, the barman hands the man the beer and says, "Excuse me, Sir, I couldn't help but notice that you have a Cornish pasty on your head."

"That's right," replies the man. "I always have a Cornish pasty on my head on a Thursday."

"But Sir, it's Friday today."

"Oh no!" says the man. "I must look a right prat."

A stranger walked into the bar and asked for a pint of beer. Now it was a very close-knit community and the locals were always suspicious of outsiders so they elected Jack from the nearby farm to find out who he was.

Some minutes later after Jack had chatted to the stranger about the weather, he asked the man what he did.

"I'm a taxidermist," replied the man, "and I've really enjoyed spending time in these parts. Yesterday I stuffed a prize-winning sheep dog, then I mounted Mrs Smith's goat and today I'm going to have a go at her old pig."

Jack returned to his mates who were dying to know what had

been said.

"It's alright, chaps," he replied to their questions. "I thought he said he was a taxi driver but in fact he's really a shepherd like us, on holiday."

A man went into a bar and ordered a gin and tonic. When it was placed before him, he exclaimed, "My goodness, an ice cube with a hole in it, that's new."

"No it isn't," commented a sullen looking man sitting next to him. "I married one."

Two men chatting over a pint.

Bob turns to John and says, "You're looking down in the dumps, what's wrong?"

"It's the wife, since she's started this high-powered job she's cut our sex down to 3 times a week."

"You're lucky," remarked Bob. "She's cut me out completely."

A man is drinking at the bar when a huge ugly woman sits down on the stool beside him. He ignores her completely and they drink away quietly for over an hour. Suddenly, the woman turns to him and slurs, "If I have another drink, I'm really going to feel it."

He replies, "To be honest, if I have another drink I probably won't mind."

★ ★ ★

A man walks into the bar with a monkey and asks for 2 pints of beer.

"We don't serve monkeys in here," replies the barman. "You'll have to go elsewhere."

"Oh come on, you can see how quiet he is, there'll be no trouble," urges the man.

Eventually the barman gives in and 2 pints are placed on the bar. However, it's not long before the monkey starts to feel the effects of the beer and he begins to get quite boisterous. All of a sudden he swings over to the snooker table, picks up the black ball and swallows it. The barman is outraged and orders them both out immediately.

"Heh, I'm really sorry, mate. That ball will have to come out at some point and then I'll bring it straight back." True to his word, a couple of days later the man returns, accompanied by the monkey on a lead and of course the black snooker ball. He hands back the ball and orders a couple of pints.

"No way," says the barman. "Who knows what trouble that monkey of yours will cause this time."

"No, no, I've got him on a lead now, nothing will happen," replies the man, so the barman serves them. The monkey sits quietly on the stool, supping his beer and occasionally taking a peanut from the dish on the bar. Each time he picks one up, he first sticks it up his backside before putting it in his mouth. The barman looks on astonished and turning to the man he asks, "What's with your monkey, why does he keep doing that with the peanuts?"

"Oh it's simple really, after the trouble with the black snooker ball he likes to test the size of the food before he eats it."

A Scottish man burst into the local pub with a completely black tongue hanging out of his mouth.

"What's happened to you?" asked one of his mates.

"A bottle of whisky fell and broke on the hot tar road," he replied.

Two penniless alcoholics are desperately seeking some way to get more booze when one of them comes up with a great idea. "Listen, mate, with our last 20p we'll buy a sausage and I'll stick it in your flies. Trust me, it can't fail." So they do as Sid suggests and then go into a bar and order 2 doubles which they soon put away. When the barman asks for the money Sid gets down on his knees and sucks the sausage sticking out of his mate's trousers.

"Ugh, you filthy buggers, get out of my bar," yells the barman, "and don't let me ever see you in here again."

The two men successfully repeat the trick all afternoon until they are so sozzled they can't stand up.

"Bloody hell," croaks Sid, "what a day...my knees ain't half sore from kneeling down so often."

"That's nothing," replies his mate. "I lost the sausage after the second pub."

A man spends the evening in the pub and by the end of the night he's so drunk he can hardly walk home. But he sets off and in a befuddled haze decides to take a short cut through the park and climb over the wall. All goes well until the final gate which is topped by sharp glass and shinning over this he badly rips his backside. By the time he gets home, he's in agony so quietly, without waking the wife, he heads for the bathroom to inspect the damage, clean up the wounds and do a bit of safety first. The next morning he crawls out of bed with a king-sized hangover and an aching arse.

"What did you get up to last night?" accused his wife. "You were horribly drunk."

"No I wasn't," he replied. "What makes you think that?"

"I'll tell you why. I found all our plasters on the bathroom mirror this morning," she retorted.

A man walks up to the bar and asks for an entendre.

"Would you like a single or a double?" asks the barmaid.

"A double please," he replies.

"OK, Sir, so yours is a large one."

222

A drunk barged into a man looking under the bonnet of his car.

"Anything wrong?" he mumbled.

"Piston broke," came the reply.

"Same here," said the drunk.

* * *

A goose waddles into a bar and asks the bartender for a dish of snails.

"This is a pub! We don't sell snails in here, only drinks" says the bartender, so the goose leaves.

The following day, the goose returns and asks for a dish of snails.

"I told you yesterday, we don't have snails, so don't waste my time," says the bartender impatiently. Again, the goose leaves.

On the next day, the goose reappears and asks for a plate of snails.

"That's it, that's bloody it," snarls the bartender. "Get out and don't ever come in here again or I'll nail your beak to the bar."

"Okay," says the goose and disappears.

But lo and behold, the goose walks in the next day, looks at the bartender and asks, "Have you got any nails?"

"NO," bellows the bartender.

"Well, in that case, have you got any snails?"

223

A dishevelled looking man walks into a bar and asks for a pint of beer.

"Now wait a minute," says the bartender suspiciously. "Let's see your money first."

"Listen mate," he replies. "I haven't got any money, but if you give me some beer, I'll stand up on the bar and fart 'Blue Suede Shoes'."

Now the bartender is intrigued by this, so he agrees. The man drinks his beer, gets up on the bar and drops his trousers. Everyone in the pub cheers loudly, but suddenly he starts to shit all over the counter.

"Aaagh!" The customers are so appalled, they immediately get up and leave.

"You fucking prat!" yells the bartender. "You said you were going to fart 'Blue Suede Shoes'."

"Now wait a minute," says the man. "Even Frank Sinatra had to clear his throat before he began to sing."

An Irishman walks into a bar with a small green man and orders two pints which they immediately drink and then he orders two more. Meanwhile, further down the bar is a man on his own and when he catches sight of the newcomers, he shouts over, "Heh, who's that little green man? He's a bit odd." Hearing this, the little green man rushes over, looks the man closely in the face and goes "Slurrpp".

"Urgh," says the man, wiping his face, "there's no need for that."

"Well, have a bit more respect then" says the Irishman, "he's a leprechaun."

An hour later and quite a few drinks later, the man shouts over again, "He's a bloody ugly bugger, isn't he?"

The little green man runs over once more and goes "Slurrpp" in his face.

This time, the man loses his temper and bellows, "If that leprechaun does it again I'll cut his knob off."

"You can't," replies the Irishman, "he hasn't got one."

"Well, how does he have a pee then?"

"He doesn't, he just goes 'Slurrpp'," comes the reply.

A man walked into a bar with a gorilla on a lead.
"I've just bought King Kong here as my new pet," he said
"and he's going to be part of the family. He'll even sleep in
the same bed as me and the wife."
"But what about the smell?" asked the barman.
"Oh, he'll just have to get used to it, I did."

A man rushes into a bar, orders four double whiskies and gulps them down immediately.

"Wow!" says the bartender. "You must be in a hurry."

"You would be too, if you had what I've got," he replies.

225

"Oh really? What's that?" he asks sympathetically.
"50p."

A man walked into the pub with a black eye. "Good heavens," exclaimed the barman, "What happened? Who gave you that?"
"No one," replied the man, "I had to fight for it."

A man walks into an empty bar and orders a drink. No one comes in so he asks the barman if he can have the TV on and the two of them watch the test match in companionable silence. England are going along nicely until the opposing team put on a fast bowler who takes two wickets in two consecutive overs. The customer turns to the barman and says, "I bet you £5 he doesn't get a wicket in this over."
Now the barman had listened to the game earlier, on the radio, and knew the bowler did get his hat-trick. "Okay mate, you're on," he says.
The next over begins and as they watch, the third wicket goes down. "Damn, damn, damn," curses the man. "I don't believe it," and he hands over £5.
Suddenly the barman feels very guilty and says, "No mate, keep your money, I listened to the game earlier on today."
"So did I," says the customer. "I just didn't think he could pull it off a second time!"

A man walks into a pub and orders three pints of beer which he drinks one by one. When he's finished, he orders another three pints and drinks them in the same way. After doing this for a whole month, the barman's curiosity gets the better of him and he asks the man why he drinks in such a fashion. "The other two pints are for my brothers who have emigrated to Australia. This is our way of remembering each other."
Then one day, the man comes in and only orders two pints. The barman hands them to him and sadly shakes his head. "I suppose this means you've lost one of your brothers, I'm very sorry."
"Oh no, not at all," replies the man, "but I've had to give up drinking."

★ ★ ★

The miserable old prat had just ordered a pint of beer when he was taken short and had to rush to the toilet. Before leaving, he spat into his pint and announced loudly, "That's mine."
A bloke next to him also spat into the pint and said, "You can keep it."

RED LIGHT AT NIGHT

A prostitute is knocked down by a car and a man runs over to help her.

"Are you alright?" he asks.

"I don't know," she replies. "I don't think I can see."

"Well, how many fingers am I holding up?" he says.

"Oh no," she wails, "I'm paralysed as well."

Definition of a prostitute:
A busy body.

A man arrives at the door of the whorehouse and asks for the services of Cara. Sure enough, Cara appears and they disappear upstairs. Afterwards he gives her £200. The next day he asks for Cara again, they do the business and he hands her another £200. This is repeated on a third and fourth day by which time Cara has become very attached to the man.

She says, "Come back tomorrow and you can have it for nothing."

"I'm sorry. I have to return to Scotland tomorrow. By the way, I know your brother and he gave me £800 to give to you."

Two prostitutes talking over a cup of tea.

"What's your day been like, Gloria?"

"Exhausting, but good business. I've climbed up and down those stairs more than 70 times today."

"Oh your poor feet!"

It was his first time in London and the American decided to search out the best brothels. At last he found one that was slightly less seedy than some of the others that he'd looked at and he went in to "be serviced".

Before taking his clothes off he thought he'd try some small talk to ease the tension he was feeling.

"Do you know I come from the other side," he said.

"Wow," she replied. "I can't wait to see this, hurry up and get your clothes off!"

The girl was asked to put down her occupation on the passport application form.

"That'll be prostitute," she replied.

"Oh no, you can't put that," exclaimed the clerk.

"How about brothel worker?" she suggested.

"No, that's no good either."

She thought for a moment and then said, "I know, put

'Poultry raiser'."
"Pardon?" he asked.
"Well, I did raise over 500 cocks last year."

A midget went into a whorehouse and demanded service. After much discussion amongst the girls, Sylvia drew the short straw and disappeared upstairs with him. But it was only a moment later when they heard a loud scream and running upstairs to the room, they found Sylvia in a swoon. Standing next to her was the midget, naked and sporting the longest dick the girls had ever seen.

After a moment of astonished silence one of the girls asked, "Wow, we've never seen anything so big before, do you mind if we touch it?"

"No, go ahead," said the midget, "but whatever you do, no sucking, I used to be 6 foot 5 inches tall."

Two dwarfs who had just done a season with the travelling circus, land up in town with wallets full of money, out for a good time. After doing a round of the bars they end up at the whorehouse and get taken upstairs by two of the working girls. Sadly, however much he tries, the first dwarf cannot get an erection so he spends the night feeling very miserable particularly as he can hear his mate next door repeating time and time again, "One, two, three up, one, two, three up."

The next morning they make their way back to the circus.
The second dwarf asks the first how it went.
"Bloody awful," he replies. "I couldn't get it to stand up to save my life. What about you?"
"Fuck nothing," he answers. "I couldn't even get onto the bed."

A man goes to a brothel, hires one of the girls and spends the next couple of hours giving her the best fuck she's ever had. He returns the following night, gets the same girl and gives a repeat performance. By the end of the third night the girl is so impressed she offers him a session on the house and it's absolutely wonderful.
"You're the most amazing thing that's ever happened to me," she tells him. "If I pay you £200 will you do it again, now?"
The man agrees but as he looks down at his small and lifeless manhood he sneers at it and says, "You're bloody good at spending it, but when it comes to earning!"

An old man goes to a whorehouse and asks how much it will be.
"Prices begin at £100," she says.
"You're putting me on," he gasps.
"Then that'll be an extra £20 on top of the price," she replies.

The same old man went back to the whorehouse a year later and staggered up to the door. He was very fragile and extremely shaky on his legs, and when Madam saw him she said, "Hey, old man, you've had it."

"Oh bugger," he replied, confused, "how much do I owe you?"

PC Jenkins was doing his nightly rounds when he discovered a woman in an alleyway. Her blouse was open, her knickers were round her ankles and she was eating a packet of sweets.

"What's going on here?" asked PC Jenkins.

"Bloody hell, has he gone?" she replied, looking around.

Throughout his teenage life, John had been warned by his God-fearing father that brothels were the ultimate places of sin and that anyone going to them would die a dreadful death.

However, one night out on a stag party John and his mates ended up in the red light district and banishing all thoughts of his father from his mind, John went into a brothel. He was taken upstairs by Madam and ushered into a bedroom where a beautiful girl lay naked on the bed. Suddenly as he looked at her, all the warnings came back to him and he cried aloud,

"Bloody hell, my dad was right, I can feel myself going stiff already."

A husband and wife went to Manchester for the day. He had a meeting in the morning and she went off to do some shopping. Now the meeting finished much earlier than expected so the man went off into the centre of town and landed up in the "better part" of the red light district. As he was passing one of the "ladies" flats, a beautiful hooker came out and before he knew what he was doing, he asked her how much she charged a session. The hooker looked at him disdainfully and told him it would be £150.
"Bloody hell, that's daylight robbery," he exclaimed, "I've only got £30," and feeling very disappointed he left to meet his wife for lunch. Just as the meal was over, the same hooker and a client entered the restaurant and on seeing the man and his wife she whispered to him as she passed.
"I hope that's taught you a lesson, that's what you get for £30."

The God of War comes to earth and enters a brothel in London where he is attracted to one girl in particular. He stays for 3 days, spending most of the time engaged in mad passionate love but then he gets a message from the heavens ordering him home. As he's about to leave, he realises he's never really spoken to the girl. He hasn't even told her his name.

"I'm Thor," he says.

"You're sore! For fuck's sake, I can't even walk," she replies angrily.

Jack was sitting at the bar looking dejectedly into his pint of beer.

"Heh, Jack, what's up?" asked the barman.

"Everything," he replied. "I got so drunk last night, I can't remember what I did, but when I woke up to find myself in bed with a woman, I naturally gave her £50."

The barman laughed. "Don't worry, mate, it happens to all of us. You'll just have to accept that you spent the money and can't remember what it was like."

"No, no, you've got me wrong," replied Jack, "the fact is that the woman in bed with me was my wife and she automatically gave me £10 change."

Having been three months up in the mountains searching for gold, the old miner suddenly struck it rich and went down into town to celebrate. He spent some time in the saloon before heading back up the main street to the local whorehouse, carrying two bottles of beer under his arm.

"I'm looking for the meanest, toughest and downright

roughest whore in town" he said to the Madam.

"You'll be wanting old Lil, then," she replied. "First on the right at the top of the stairs."

So upstairs he went and banged on the door.

"Are you the meanest, toughest and downright roughest whore in town?" he yelled as he opened the door.

"I sure am," she said, grinning, and with that she stripped off, bent over and grabbed her ankles.

"Heh! How do you know that's my favourite position?" he asked.

"I don't," she replied, "but I thought you might like to open those two beers first."

A man knocks at the door of a whore house and asks the Madam for "a girl, please".

Now this particular Madam is an unscrupulous bitch and when she sees how naive the man is, she reckons she'll get away with giving him an inflatable doll and he'll never know the difference.

But after a few minutes the young man appears.

"Everything alright?" she asks.

"Well, I don't know," he replies. "I bit her on the bum, she farted and flew straight out of the window."

The man was out of the door without paying before the whore had a chance to stop him. "If it's a boy, name it after me. "Lucky," he shouted arrogantly as he disappeared round the corner.

"And if it itches, name it after me 'eczema'," bellowed the whore angrily.

Arthur was such an unlucky man. One day he approached a prostitute and she said she had a headache.

An old man knocked on the door of the local brothel and spoke to the Madam.

"I've got plenty of money and I want me a girl," he said, "but she must have VD."

"Okay old man," said the Madam and she directed him to a room upstairs where a girl was waiting, lying stark naked on the bed.

"Do you have VD?" asked the old man.

"I certainly don't," she protested.

So the old man sent her away and asked for someone else.

"Listen, Elsie," said Madam, "Go and see to the old man in Room 7 and if he asks, say you've got the clap."

Elsie went off to Room 7, confirmed that she had VD and serviced the old man for half an hour. At the end of the session, she told him that she had a confession to make.

"I don't really have VD, old man," she said.
The man smiled sadly and replied, "Well, you do now."

The prostitute was so fed up with her client's fumbling that she was forced to put him in her place.

Did you hear what happened when the nymphomaniac went to the library?
She got a book out called "How to Hump" and didn't realise until she got home that it was volume 4 of the encyclopaedia.

PILLAR OF SOCIETY

One of Johnny's Dad's greatest mysteries was "how is it, as a young man, you set out to become one of society's pillars, but end up as one of society's pillocks?" Johnny himself wanted to be a doctor but failed the interview when he was asked to show his testimonials. And although he thinks a knighthood is something that comes with a fancy pair of pyjamas, he would like another gong – the first one he got was when he was booed off at the Comedy Store.

HEALTHY BEHAVIOUR

Did you hear about the man who went to the chiropodist's and put his willy on the table?
When the chiropodist told him it wasn't a foot, he replied, "I know, but I'm proud it's 11 inches."

"A packet of condoms please," said the man to the sales assistant.
"What size, sir?" she asked.
"Er...I don't know."
"Well, that's no problem," she replied. "If you go into the other room, you'll find a board with a selection of different holes. Just pop your todger in them until you find the right size."
So the man did as he was told, little realising that every time he tried a different hole, the sales assistant was on the other side fondling it. Eventually, he was satisfied he had found the correct size, so returned to the counter.
"Everything alright, sir?" she asked.
"Couldn't be better," he replied, "but forget the condoms, just sell me the board."

The man rang the local mental institution and asked to speak to the patient in room 24.

"I'm sorry, sir, room 24 is unoccupied at present."

"Whoopee," shouted the man. "I did it, I escaped."

The poor man had a dreadful medical problem, so he went along to the chemist to see if they could help him. Unfortunately, the shop was owned by two spinsters, but it was too late to walk out, so blushing profusely, he explained that he had a permanent erection and what could they give him for it.

"Just a moment, Sir" and the two women went into the back room to confer.

A couple of minutes later, they returned smiling happily.

"Okay, we've talked it over and we can offer you a half partnership in the shop and £1,000 cash."

The local Mayor decided to do something useful for the community so went along to the sperm bank to make a donation. "Have you been before?" asked the receptionist.

"I believe I have," replied the Mayor. "You've probably got my notes from last time."

"Oh yes," replied the girl. "You're going to need some help so I'll put you in our category D area."

"Wait a minute, what do you mean, category D! I don't need

any help!"
"I'm sorry, Sir, but it says in your notes that you're a clueless wanker."

Jack's wife went along to the optician's for her annual check-up.
"Right," said the optician. "Can you read the bottom line?"
After a few moments she shook her head.
"OK, try the next line."
Again she shook her head. This went on until they got to the largest letter at the top but she still shook her head. By this time the optician was so frustrated he unzipped his trousers, pulled out his willy and shouted, "Well, can you see this?"
"Oh yes," she replied.
"Now I know what the trouble is," he said. "You're cock-eyed."

To assess Pete's state of mind the psychiatrist told him he was going to make some random marks on the paper and Pete was to tell him what he saw.
After the first mark Pete replied, "That's Madonna in the nude."
For the second mark he said, "That's my next door neighbour stark naked," and for the third mark, "That's the whole of my wife's knitting circle with no clothes on."

The psychiatrist looked up exasperated.

"The trouble with you, Pete, is that you're obsessed with sex."

"Get off," retorted Pete angrily. "You're the one drawing the dirty pictures."

Did you hear about the psychiatrist who kept his wife under the bed?
He thought she was a little potty.

A very rich woman reaches middle age and decides to have a face-lift to keep her looking young. She goes along to the most famous and wickedly expensive surgeon in town and he explains he has discovered a new and revolutionary technique.

"Once I have performed the operation, I will put two little screws behind each ear and whenever you see a little wrinkle appear, you just gently turn the screws and it will disappear." The technique is a wonderful success and for over 10 years the woman keeps a wrinkle-free face by turning the screws when necessary. However, one day she notices she has bags under her eyes but when she turns the screws, no matter how many times, the bags will not go away. In a blind panic she rushes back to the surgeon.

"Look what's happened," she wails. "I can't get rid of them."

The surgeon replies, "Madam, you have used the screws so much that those bags under your eyes are your breasts and if you continue to turn the screws, you'll end up with a beard."

"I am very sorry to say that I have two bad pieces of news for you," said the doctor to his patient.
"Oh dear, what is it?" asked the patient.
"You have only 24 hours to live," came the reply.
"Oh no, what other piece of bad news could there be?"
"I tried to get you on the phone all day yesterday."

DOCTOR'S ORDERS

A man went to the doctor feeling very depressed.
"What you need," said the doctor, "is some companionship.
Go out and find a girl who likes to do the same things as you
do."
"But doc, why would I want a girl who likes whistling at other
girls!"

A 20-stone man went to the doctor's complaining of a bad
chest. The doctor examined him with his stethoscope and
then asked the man to strip off completely.
"Would you mind getting down on all fours and crawling
over to the window for me, please?" he asked.
The man did as he was requested.
"Good, good," murmured the doctor.
"Now would you mind crawling over to the wall on your
right. That's it, just between the chair and the filing cabinet."
The doctor scratched his head thoughtfully. "Thank you
very much, Mr White, you may get dressed now."
Once he'd put his clothes back on, the man asked the doctor
for his verdict.
"Oh you're quite right, you've got a bad chest so I'll give you
a prescription for some antibiotics."
"But doctor, how on earth did crawling around the room

246

like that help your diagnosis?"

"Oh it didn't," replied the doctor, "but I'm having a pale pink settee delivered next week and I was just interested to know where the best place to put it might be."

"It's no good, Mabel, I can't find anything wrong with you, it must be the effects of drinking," said the doctor.

"Well, in that case I'll come back when you're sober!" exclaimed the woman.

A very obese man went to the doctor's and was told he would have to lose at least 7 stone.

"It's no good," wailed the man. "I've tried all sorts of diets and they never work."

"Well, this one is different," said the doctor. "You will take nothing by mouth, everything you eat will be through your rectum."

A month went by and the man went back to the doctors looking very happy.

"Well done, you've lost nearly 4 stone, carry on like this and you'll soon be down to the correct weight. Do you have any problems?"

"None at all," said the man. "I'll see you in a month's time."

As the man walked to the door, the doctor noticed that he was walking in an odd way.

"Are you sure there's nothing wrong?" asked the doctor. "You seem to be walking in a curious way."

"No, everything's fine, doc," said the man. "I'm just chewing some bubble gum."

"Doctor, doctor, I'm so embarrassed, I've got several holes in my willy and when I go for a pee it sprinkles out all over me and over anyone standing close by. Please say you can do something."

The doctor considered the man for a few minutes and then wrote something down on a card.

"Here," he said, "take this card, on it is the name of a man who can help you."

"Oh thanks, doc, will he be able to cure me?"

"No, but he's one of the country's finest flute players and he'll show you how to hold it properly."

At first Johnny was embarrassed to find a lady doctor waiting for him in the surgery. She asked him to strip and then began examining him. As she put her soft, gentle hands on his body she said, "Say 99 please."

Johnny smiled and then as slowly as he could began 1... 2... 3...

A man suffering from constipation was given a course of suppositories by his GP. But a week later he was back complaining they hadn't worked.

"Are you sure you've been taking them regularly?" asked the doctor.

"Of course I bloody well have," he answered angrily. "What do you think I've been doing, sticking them up my arse?"

"Oh doctor, doctor," said the embarrassed woman. "I think I suffer from being sexually perverted."

"Can you tell me about it?" asked the doctor kindly. "I'm sure it's not as bad as you think."

"I can't possibly," she replied, blushing madly. "It's too awful."

After a few minutes of gentle persuasion the doctor eventually said, "You know, many people have strange perversions, even I do. So if you show me yours, then I'll show you mine."

"Well…" she stammered. "I like my bottom to be kissed."

"Oh goodness, that's not much," said the doctor. "Pop round behind the screen and then I'll show you mine."

A couple of minutes later, the doctor called her round and he's sitting there looking very smug.

"I thought you were going to show me your perversion," she whined.

"Of course, look, I've shat in your handbag."

249

There are only two men in the doctor's waiting room. One has his arm bandaged up and the second is covered in food – potatoes in his hair, a lamb chop sticking out of his pocket, gravy running down his trousers and peas up his nose. The second man turns to the first and asks him what happened.

"Oh it's my own fault," he replies. "I was looking at this beautiful girl instead of watching where I was going. I tripped over a step and I think I might have broken my arm. What about you?"

"Oh it's nothing much, I'm just not eating properly."

A man went to the doctor's feeling run down.

"What you need is a holiday," said the doctor. "You need to get away from the routine, could you go abroad?"

"I sure could," replied the man. "What's she like?"

★ ★ ★

A woman took her son down to the doctor's surgery.
"Doctor, tell me please, can a boy of 13 take out his own appendix?" she demanded.
"Indeed not," said the doctor.
"There you are, I told you so," she yelled at her son, "now put it back immediately."

A couple went to the doctor's and asked him if he minded watching them have sexual intercourse. The doctor was used to odd requests so he agreed and after it was over he charged them £35. The following week they returned and asked him again. He assured them that there was nothing wrong with their technique, but they were so insistent that he relented. Again, he charged them £35.

However, when they came back a third time, the doctor became very suspicious.

"Why are you doing this?" he asked.

"You're doing us a big favour, doc," they said. "I'm married, my girlfriend lives with her mum, and the hotels are very expensive. If we come here it only costs us £35 and I can claim it back on my private health insurance."

★ ★ ★

A married couple went along to the doctor's because their love life was very unsatisfactory. The doctor began by asking, "Mr Jones, do you shrink from lovemaking?"

"No," he replied. "I've always been this small."

A woman goes to a sleazy back street doctor complaining that she doesn't feel very well. Before she can say any more, he tells her to go into the other room, strip off and lay down on the bed. When he comes in, he's so taken with her beauty that he immediately starts to fondle her whole body.

"Don't worry, this is quite normal," he simpers. "I expect you know what I'm doing?"

"I suppose you're checking for anything unusual," she replies.

"That's right," he responds, and then quick as a flash he strips off, lays on top of her and starts making love.

"Do you know what I'm doing now?" he asks.

"Oh yes," she replies. "You're getting herpes. That's what I was trying to tell you earlier."

The doctor was so excited. "This is absolutely amazing. You will become a celebrity and I will be interviewed in every medical journal around the world. You realise, Mr Lester, that you're the first man ever to become pregnant."

But the man did not share the doctor's joy.

"Oh dear, what shall I do? I'm not married. What will my parents think? How will the neighbours react?"

"It's no good, Mr Weeks, you'll have to go on a healthier diet. Try eating more fruit," said the doctor.
"But doctor, I do have a lot of fruit. Why! I have two slices of lemon in every gin and tonic."

A woman went to the doctor's with her son because she was concerned that his penis was too small and not growing normally.
"Nothing to worry about," replied the doctor. "Every night, before he goes to bed, give him a cup of hot milk and put in a teaspoon of this special B16 powder. That'll soon put things right."
A few evenings later, the little boy walked into the kitchen to find his mum putting three tablespoons of the powder into a mug of hot milk. "But Mum," said the boy, "the doctor only said a teaspoon."
"Oh this is not for you," she replied, "this is for your father."

"Doctor," asked the young pregnant woman. "My baby's due any day, can you recommend the best position for delivering it?"

"Well, Mrs Goodly, the position most women choose is exactly the same position as when they conceived."

"Oh no! For me that's the 10.50 train from Paddington to Penzance."

"Doctor, help me please, I can hardly walk, my backside's killing me!"

"Mmm, bend over and we'll see what's wrong," replied the doctor.

"Aah, I can see the problem, you've got a bunch of flowers stuck up there."

"Thank goodness for that," smiled the man. "Is there a message with them?"

The doctor examined the wife's husband thoroughly before he turned to her and said, "I'm sorry, I don't like the look of your husband."

"Neither do I," she replied, "but at least he's useful around the house."

"Doctor, doctor, please help me," begged the man. "I can't satisfy my wife, I think my penis is too small."

The doctor replied, "I think we can do something about that. Do you drink cider?"

"Yes."

"Mmm, cider tends to keep it small. What you need to drink are bottles of stout. Try that for a month and then come back and see me."

A month later, the man returned to the surgery looking very happy.

"Aah, I can see it worked, you're drinking the stout."

"It's worked alright, the sex is great now," replied the man. "But I don't drink the stout, I give it to the wife."

★ ★ ★

A man goes to the surgery feeling sick, but the doctor is unable to diagnose what's wrong with him, so he takes some blood tests and tells him to return the following week. However, he's too ill to leave the house so his wife goes along to get the results.

"Oh dear, oh dear," says the doctor, shaking his head, "it seems I have two patients by the name of Jack Brown, they've both had blood tests this week and the tests have been muddled up. It means your husband either has VD or Alzheimer's disease."

The poor wife is very distressed.

"What shall I do?" she asks.

"Don't worry, it's quite simple," replies the doctor. "Take

your husband on a long journey, go by bus and train, then leave him there and see if he can find his way home. If he does get home alright, then don't let him fuck you."

A very small woman went to the doctor's complaining that her pussy hurt. After a thorough examination, the doctor looked puzzled.

"Does it hurt all the time?" he asked.

"Oh no, just when it's raining."

"Okay, well, next time it's wet, come and see me."

A few days later the woman turned up at the surgery and the doctor examined her again.

"Ah ha, now I see what the matter is. Nurse, hand me my scissors please."

After a couple of minutes, the little woman stood up, overjoyed that the pain had gone."

"What caused it?" she asked.

He replied, "Your wellingtons were too high. Once I'd trimmed an inch off all round, the problem was solved."

As the woman walked into the surgery, the doctor greeted her. "Hello, Mrs Smith, would you mind going over to the window and sticking your tongue out?"

"Why?"

"Because I can't stand the person living opposite."

"Every time I sneeze, I have an orgasm," said the girl to her doctor.
"What do you take for it?" he asked.
"Pepper."

"Doctor, doctor, please help me, I can't stop farting. The only good thing is, they don't smell."
"Okay," said the doctor, opening the window," it will mean a small operation."
"What! Will it be painful?"
"No, no, just an operation on your nose. Once we've cured that, we'll see to the other problem."

A man is suffering very badly from severe headaches, dizziness and spots before the eyes.
"I'm sorry to say," said the doctor, "that you have got an infection in your testicles and unless you have them removed, the symptoms will spread."
Unwilling to accept this dreadful diagnosis, the man consults two other doctors but they both give the same opinion. So resigned to his fate, the man has both testicles removed.
Some days later, in an effort to cheer himself up, he decides to go shopping. He visits the most exclusive gentlemen's

outfitters for miles around.

"Ah yes," says the tailor. "You're a 34 inch waist, 32 inch inside leg and 15?" collar size."

"That's very impressive" says the man. "How can you be so accurate?"

"Years of training, Sir," replies the tailor. "I also know that you are a 40 inch chest, take size 11 inch in shoes and wear medium sized underpants."

"Absolutely correct," says the man, "except for the underpants. I take a small size."

"Then may I suggest you change the size, Sir, otherwise you'll eventually start to suffer from severe headaches, dizziness and spots before the eyes."

A woman goes to the doctor complaining that two green marks have appeared on the inside of her thighs.

"Mmm," says the doctor, puzzled, "now what can that be..."
He thinks for a while and then a smile crosses his face. "You don't happen to go out with a gypsy, do you?" he asks.

"Why, yes, I do."

"Well, that's the answer. Tell your boyfriend that his earrings are not real gold!"

"Doctor, doctor, I think I may be impotent. When I try and make love to my wife nothing happens."

The doctor thinks for a moment and then says, "Make an appointment for both you and your wife to come to the surgery and I'll see what I can do."

So the following week they both turn up at the surgery. The doctor takes the wife into another room and asks her to undress. Then he asks her to walk up and down, twirl around and jump in the air.

"Thank you very much, Mrs Smith, you can get dressed now."

The doctor goes back into the other room and takes the husband to one side.

"Don't worry, Mr Smith, there's nothing wrong with you, your wife doesn't give me a hard-on either."

The beautiful curvaceous blonde patient was whispering frantically. "Oh please kiss me again, please kiss me again."

"I don't know," replied the doctor, "it's not right, I really shouldn't be fucking you at all."

The world-famous doctor was at his wit's end. Never before had he been unable to find out what was wrong with a patient, but this man had him beaten. On five separate occasions, the doctor had examined him but could find nothing wrong.

There was only one thing to do. The next time the man

came in he told him to urinate into a bowl. So the patient did as he was ordered. Then the doctor told him to shit into the same bowl, which the patient also did. Stirring the foul mixture together, the doctor made the man swallow a large jug full of the stuff and the man immediately vomited all over the floor. "Ah ah" shouted the doctor triumphantly. "Now I know what's wrong, you have an upset stomach."

★ ★ ★

A girl goes to the doctor's complaining of a strange mark on her chest. When she shows it to the doctor, he sees a letter C imprinted on her breasts.

"How did you get this?" he enquires.

"It's my boyfriend. He wears a medallion around his neck which has a C on the end of it, representing the university he goes to – Cambridge. And when we make love, it presses into me."

"Okay, well use this cream twice a day and it'll soon go away," says the doctor.

The next day, another girl visits the surgery. She's complaining of a strange mark on her chest which is like the letter O.

"My boyfriend wears a silver O round his neck representing Oxford University and when we have sex, the weight of his body leaves a mark" she explains.

"I know just what you need," says the doctor, and he gives her some cream. On the third day, another girl comes in to see him. This one has the imprint of an M on her chest.

"I know what that is," says the doctor confidently. "I bet your boyfriend goes to Manchester University."

"Oh no," she replies, "but I do have a girlfriend at Wolverhampton Tech."

"Doctor, doctor," said the simple old woman, "I must have a hysterectomy, I really must."

"But why?" asked the puzzled doctor.

"Because I've twenty grandchildren already and I don't want any more!"

The old man hobbled into the doctor's surgery and pleaded, "Doctor, please help me, you've got to give me something to lower my sex drive."

"Come on now, Mr Bates," replied the doctor, looking at the doddering old man. "Your sex drive is all in the head."

"That's what I mean. I need something to lower it."

"Doctor, doctor, is it alright to masturbate?" asked the concerned man.

"Everything in moderation," replied the doctor.

"Is four times a day alright?"

"Well, that's quite a lot, why don't you get married, that's a much better idea."

"I am married."

"And is everything fine in bed?"

"It's great."

"Then why do you need to masturbate so much?"

"She's such a spoil-sport. She doesn't like to do it during mealtimes."

"A man goes into the doctor's and says. "Every time I look in the mirror, I see myself as old and haggard."

"Well at least there's nothing wrong with your eyesight," replies the doctor.

DOWN IN THE MOUTH

A woman walked into the dentist very nervously and said, "I'd rather have a baby than have my teeth checked." "Okay," said the dentist, "if that's what you want, then I'll have to adjust the chair."

A man went to the dentist with a raging toothache.
"It'll have to come out immediately," said the dentist, taking hold of his drill.
The patient grabbed hold of the dentist's balls and replied, "We're not going to hurt each other, are we?"

It was the annual conference for dentists and dental companies and one of the awards went to Matthew Slick for best salesman of the year. He had sold a record quantity of White's dental mouthwash. Some time later, after he'd been presented with his award, a colleague asked him for the secret of his success.

"Oh it's quite simple really," said Matthew. "For the past six months I've been setting up a mobile stall at the major

London railway stations during their busy rush-hour periods. The stall has been giving away free samples of a new meat paste. When people ask me what it contains, I tell them it has venison, herbs and bull droppings. As they start to spit it out, that's when I ask them if they'd like to buy a bottle of White's dental mouthwash."

HOSPITAL HABITS

It was Monday morning and the great but absent-minded rectal surgeon was on his rounds. Halfway round the ward the nurse nudged him and whispered in his ear.

"Sir, you have a suppository behind your left ear."

"Oh damn," cursed the surgeon, "that means some bum's got my pencil."

A gorgeous shapely girl was lying naked in a hospital bed with just a sheet covering her. Suddenly a young man came in, pulled back the sheet and examined her closely.

"What's the verdict?" she asked.

He replied, "I don't know, you'll have to ask the doctor that, I'm only the window cleaner."

"I'm sorry, Sir," said the hospital, "but your wife has suffered severe facial injuries and is in need of some plastic surgery. It will cost £3,000 and we will need to take some skin off your backside."

"No problem," replied the husband, so the operation went ahead and was a great success.

A couple of weeks later, the man received a telephone call

265

from the plastic surgeon.

"You've given me £500 too much," he said.

"Oh no," he replied, "the extra is for the immense pleasure I get out of seeing my mother-in-law kiss my arse."

"Your new hand has taken perfectly," said the doctor, "everything's connected up well, so what's the problem?"

"Well, doc, it's not a problem most of the time, but you gave me a female hand and every time I go for a piss, it won't let go."

Two nurses enjoy a good night out but return to the nurses' home after the doors have been locked. They decide to climb up the drainpipe and crawl through an open window. Half-way up, one nurse turns to the other giggling and says, "Doing this makes me feel like a burglar."

"Same here" replied her friend, "but where will we find two burglars at this time of night?"

"Oh Carol, you'll never guess what I've just seen," said the plain nurse to the pretty nurse. "The man in cubicle 7 has 'NOON' tattooed on his willy."

"Oh no," replied Carol, "it's not NOON, its Northampton."

One of the fielders got hit in the crotch by a cricket ball, the pain was so severe he collapsed unconscious on the ground and woke up in hospital.

"Hey doc," he croaked, "am I alright? Will I be able to play again?"

The doctor replied, "Yes, you'll be able to play again... that's if you've got a women's team at the club."

A man went to the doctor's with a bad wrist and after a quick examination, he was transferred to the accident and emergency unit at the local hospital. Immediately on getting there, the nurse asked him for a urine sample which he thought was a very odd thing to ask for, considering it was his wrist that hurt. However, nurse insisted, so he did as she wished. Fifteen minutes later, he was ushered in to see the doctor who told him he had dislocated his wrist.

"Don't tell me you learnt that from the urine sample," laughed the man.

"Oh yes we did," insisted the doctor, "there have been such great developments in medicine and we now have a fool-proof way of diagnosing many complaints just by taking a urine sample."

After the man was patched up, he left for home. An appointment was made to see him in six weeks' time, when he had to bring along another sample. On the day of the next visit, the man decided to test just how good the new method was so he peed in the jar, got his wife and daughter to do the same, as well as the cat, and also wanked into it. This time, the analysis took much longer, but eventually he got in to see the doctor.

"Well? What's the verdict?" he asked.

The doctor looked at him very seriously and replied, "Your wrist is much better, but your wife has VD, your daughter is pregnant, the cat has fleas and if you continue wanking, your wrist will worsen."

Did you hear about the gay ENT surgeon?
He was known as the Queer nose and throat specialist!

A man visited a plastic surgeon with a badly damaged penis. "What happened to you?" asked the surgeon.

"It's like this," said the man, blushing madly. "I live on a caravan park next to this beautiful lady. And she really does turn me on. Each night, I watch her take a sausage from the fridge, stick it in a hole in the caravan floor and then she sits on it and does the business."

"So how did you get involved?" asked the surgeon.

"Well doc, I thought a long time about this and decided it was such a waste. So one night, I crawled under the caravan, took the sausage away and substituted my dick."

"So what happened?"

"Everything was going fine until there was a knock at her door. She jumped up and tried to kick the sausage under the table!"

A man had his penis cut off in a gruesome industrial accident but he was fortunate enough to qualify for a penis transplant. After the operation had been carried out and the man had come round from the anaesthetic, he asked the surgeon how it went.

"Well, there's good news and bad news," replied the surgeon. "The good news is that the operation was a complete success and you are now the proud owner of an exceptionally good member. But the bad news is that your hand has rejected it."

ON THE MOVE

"I hope you don't mind me asking," said the young American girl to the Scotsman, "but I've often wondered what you wear under your kilt."

The Scotsman replied that if she was really curious to know, then she could put her hand up his kilt and find out for herself.

So, a little apprehensively, she did as he suggested and put her hand under his kilt.

"Aaagh, it's gruesome," she screamed, quickly removing her hand.

"Aye, it is that, lass," replied the Scotsman, "and if you put your hand up again, you'll find it's gruesome more."

The hotel was holding a prestigious convention. After the first day of meetings, people were going back to their rooms to freshen up for dinner. The lifts were packed solid.

"Which floors please?" called out the attendant.

A voice from the back shouted "Ballroom" and a woman just in front of him replied, "Do forgive me, I didn't know I was crushing you that much!"

The plane's engines are failing and the pilot informs the passengers that the situation is very serious, their only hope is finding a place good enough to try a crash landing.

Most of the passengers turn to the alcohol trolley, determined to get so pissed they won't feel the pain, but one man alone asks the black stewardess if he can sleep with her. At first she's outraged, but then decides that making love is as good a way as any of spending her last few minutes alive. So they retire to the back of the plane and get down to it. After a moment or so, she asks him why he chose her instead of getting drunk like the rest of them.

"Well, I've always been told that the only part of the plane which survives a crash is the black box, so I reckoned I'd be in it when the plane went down."

The big game hunter, out on safari, came across a naked woman stretched out on the ground.
He said, "Excuse me, Miss, are you game?"
"I sure am," she said.
So he shot her.

A businessman books into a country hotel, asks for breakfast at 8.30 and requests a girl to come to his room after dinner that night. "That's outrageous!" says the wife. "What sort of hotel does he think we are running? Go and tell him, Fred."

But her husband thinks it's a lot of fuss about nothing and tells her so.

"Okay, if you won't go, then I will", and she disappears up to his room.

Some time later, the man appears in the bar for a nightcap and seeing the husband, he comments, "My goodness, that was quite a woman you sent up. I like the hard-to-get type, it's more fun, particularly in the end when they surrender."

Staying overnight at a prestigious hotel, the couple were disturbed by the dreadful noise coming from downstairs. The man was soon on the phone to reception.

"What's all this noise about, I've spent a lot of money coming here and I don't expect to be kept awake all night by that racket."

"I'm very sorry, Sir," said the receptionist, "they're holding the Policeman's Ball."

"Well, tell them to leave the bugger alone, so we can get some sleep."

A vicar booked into an hotel for the night on his way back from a convention. After supper, he got talking to the woman behind the bar, called Maisie, and invited her up to his room when she'd finished work.

At one o'clock, there was a knock on his door and she

walked in carrying a bottle of champagne. By the time it was half empty, they were in bed enjoying themselves. Suddenly, she turned to him and said, "I'm not sure this is right, you being a man of the cloth."

"No need to worry," he replied. "I read about it in this Gideon Bible here."

"What do you mean?" she asked.

"Well, on the inside front cover it says, 'If you want a good fuck, ask Maisie in the bar.' "

A seaman is given 10 days' shore leave in Thailand and every night he hits the high spots – drinking and whoring non-stop. However, towards the end of his leave he realises there's something wrong with him so he goes to see a European doctor.

"I'm afraid you have picked up a new and virulent sexual disease. It means you will have to have your penis surgically removed."

Horrified, the man goes to see another European doctor but the diagnosis is the same.

Walking slowly back to his ship, he loses his way down the many back alleys and discovers the premises of an old Thai doctor. Desperate for better news, he goes in and is examined thoroughly.

"You do not need to have your penis surgically removed," says the doctor "that is just a way for these foreigners to make more money."

Overjoyed, the man replies, "Then everything is going to be alright?"

"Oh no," says the doctor. "I mean your penis will just drop off on its own in a few days' time."

A professor and a young girl find themselves travelling in the same railway carriage as they race through England's green and pleasant land. The girl starts to get aroused when she notices all the animals in the fields are humping each other and she asks the professor how they become attracted.

"That's very simple, my dear," replies the professor, "the female gives off a sexual odour which tells the male that she is interested."

The professor goes back to reading his book and they soon arrive at their destination.

"I hope we meet again one day," he says as they part company.

"Only if you get your sense of smell back," she retorts.

Three hunters out on safari were caught by a tribe of ferocious indians.

"You will all die," said the chief, "but you will die in a manner reflecting what you were on earth. What did you do?" he asked the first hunter.

"I was a surgeon," he replied.

"OK, you will die by having your penis amputated."
He turned to the second man and asked him the same question.
"I was a fireman."
"OK, you will die by having your penis burnt off."
"And you?" said the chief to the third hunter.
"Oh, I was a lollipop man," replied the man, smiling.

"Ladies and Gentlemen, we're only 20 minutes from landing, I hope you've enjoyed the flight and in a few moments I'll ask you to fasten your seat belts," said the pilot. However, he forgot to turn the microphone off and the passengers then heard him turn to his co-pilot and say, "Well, Jack, I can't wait to get down. I shall finish up the paperwork and then take that gorgeous new air stewardess back to my place for a good shagging."
Hearing this, the poor air stewardess blushed madly and rushed up the aisle to warn him, but on the way, she tripped over a bag and fell sprawling on the floor. An old lady sitting next to the aisle, bent down and whispered to her.
"It's all right, dear, you've got plenty of time. He's got to finish his paperwork first."

A tough looking cowboy stormed into the saloon, guns swinging from both hips, and bellowed, "Whoever pinched

my horse, the fucking bastard better have it back here in 5 minutes or I'll be forced to do what I did in Denver."
He sat down, had a drink and after 5 minutes went to the saloon doors and sure enough, the horse had been returned. As the man was about to leave, the barman beckoned him over.
"Before you go, what did happen in Denver?"
"I had to walk," he replied.

A taxi driver was taking an attractive girl home when his cab failed. He got out to see what the trouble was and shortly afterwards the girl got out too and peered over his shoulder.
"Do you want a screwdriver?" she asked.
"Don't mind if I do," he replied. "Just a moment while I close the bonnet."

I'm sorry, Sir, all our en-suite rooms are taken. Do you mind sharing a bath with another of the male guests?" said the hotel receptionist to the simple man.
"Not at all," he replied, "as long as he keeps to his end of the bath."

A man was driving along in a remote part of Scotland when he was flagged down by a really ugly looking woman. She called to him, "Come and make love to me or drive on to success."

It wasn't difficult decision and the man carried on. Sometime later he was flagged down by another woman, slightly better than the first, and she called out to him, "Come and make love to me or drive on to success."

The man continued on and over the next 20 miles he was flagged down by 4 different women, each one better than the one before. The fourth woman was the most attractive he'd ever seen but when she cried, "Let's make love now or you can drive on to success" he reluctantly passed her by in anticipation of the more beautiful girl he would meet next. However, as he came round a sharp bend in the road he was brought to a stop by a huge ape-like looking man who was so dirty and smelly it was impossible to get near him.

"Who are you?" asked the man.

"Oh I'm Cess," he replied, winking.

A middle-aged man and a woman with a baby found themselves travelling in the same railway carriage.

"What a bonny baby," commented the man.

"Thank you," replied the woman. "She's very special to me because I waited for over 10 years of marriage before she came along."

"Well, your patience has been rewarded," he said. "A bit like

277

me really. I breed racing pigeons but it took me more than
15 years before I started producing champions."
"Why's that?" asked the woman.
"Oh, I finally changed the cock."
"Really! That's what I did," she replied.

It is the highlight of the holiday. The small group of tourists
are off on safari which is to last two days. After travelling
many miles the first day, they make camp in a small clearing,
have some supper and retire to their tents. However, in the
middle of the night a gorilla wanders into the camp and
walks into a tent where a young, shy girl is sleeping. Before
she knows what is happening he's picked her up and given
her a good rogering before disappearing as quickly as he
came. The sound of her cries alert the rest of the party and
when she tells them what has happened, they immediately
take her to hospital, where she spends a week in a state of
shock. A little while later, the leader of the safari comes to
see her to find out how she's coping.
"It's awful," she replies tearfully. "I've heard nothing from
him, no phone call, no letter, nothing."

A simple man was sitting at the bar, chuckling into his pint of
beer. Eventually the barman was so curious he came over to
ask what was so funny.

"It's my wife," laughed the man. "She's gone off to Spain for a holiday but she really is so thick. I watched her pack her suitcase and she put in 5 packets of condoms! And she doesn't even have a willy."

It's been 3 months since the sailor was stranded alone on the desert island. Then without warning he sees a barrel floating to shore, carrying a gorgeous naked lady.
"I bet I can guess what you want," she says, smiling.
"Oh no," he gasps happily, "don't tell me you've got rum in that barrel."

The taxi was travelling at over 90 mph through the middle of the town when the male passenger tapped the driver on the shoulder.
"Heh, what's all the rushing for? Slow down a bit."
"Sorry, mate, I thought I heard someone shout 'faster, faster',", said the taxi driver.
"Well, you heard right, but she wasn't talking to you!" came the reply.

Three blokes landed up at their ski resort a day early and discovered their rooms would not be ready until the

279

···

following day. The only accommodation available that night was one room with a large king sized bed. The three men decided they could put up with sharing a bed for one night so they booked in. The next morning the man on the far left said, "I had such a strange night, I dreamt I was wanking like mad all night, yet it seemed to be happening without me using my hands."

"Bloody hell," said the man on the far right, I had exactly the same dream, that's really weird. How about you, Johnny? Did you also have that dream?"

"No, mate," replied Johnny, "I just dreamt I was skiing all night!"

A dedicated professor of music decided to go deep into the African jungle to test his theory that wild animals could be tamed by playing them beautiful music. Sure enough, his theory proved to be true. As he began playing a beautiful piece of classical music on his violin, he soon had an appreciative audience – two giraffes, three snakes, four zebras and a host of monkeys. All of a sudden, a lion roared into the middle of them and bit off the professor's head.

"Why did you do that?" complained the other animals. "That was beautiful music and you've gone and spoilt it."

The lion put a paw to his ear and said "What?"

During his holiday in Germany, the man met a high-class prostitute, they had a few drinks and then went back to her place where sex was performed all over the house and in every position possible. The next morning he thanked her profusely for such good German hospitality and headed for the door.

"Just a moment," she said. "What about the marks?"

"Oh right," he said. "I'd give it nine out of 10."

Two men are sitting opposite each other in a railway compartment. The younger of the two asks his companion if he has the time. There is no answer. Again and again he asks but gets no reply. Eventually the man taps him on the knee and shouts, "Do you have the time please?"

"Yes, it's half past three," replies the older man.

"Thank you, but why did you take so long to answer?"

"Well, it's like this. Once I'd told you the time, we'd get talking, become friends, find we had something in common ... then I'd invite you to visit us, you'd meet our beautiful daughter, fall in love with her and want to get married. And to be honest with you, I don't want to have son-in-law who hasn't even got a watch."

An old, smelly drunken man gets on a bus and sits down next to a very refined middle-aged woman. She turns to him and

281

says contemptuously, "My man, you are going straight to hell."

He jumps up immediately and shouts to the conductor, "Fuck me, I'm on the wrong bus!"

A blind man stood at the edge of the pavement, waiting to cross the road, when his guide dog weed all down the side of his leg.

The man immediately took a biscuit from his pocket and gave it to the dog. An onlooker turned to him and said, "That's very good of you, considering he just soaked your leg."

"Not really," replied the blind man. "I'm just finding out where his mouth is so that I can kick him in the balls."

A group of tourists were on a coach trip through California when the guide's voice came over the microphone.

"If you look to your left you'll see we're just passing the most famous whorehouse in the West."

"But why?" replied one of the sightseers.

How can you tell if a motorcyclist is happy?
By seeing all the insects on his teeth.

On a walking holiday over Dartmoor, a man comes across a naked youth tied to a tree.

"Oh thank goodness you've found me," exclaims the youth. "I was out for a day's walk when I got attacked by two bastards who robbed me of everything I had, and even took my clothes. It's been a bloody nightmare."

The walker looked at the boy and smiled.

"It's just not your day, is it, son?" he said, unbuckling his trousers.

Three men get captured in the jungle by cannibals and are taken back to the big Chief who immediately gets out his penis and tells them that if their 3 penises together can match his, then they will be set free. Now the cannibal chief has a 22 inch donger so the first man gets his out and it measures 11 inches. The second man reveals his and it's 9 inches. Only another 2 inches are needed so the men are feeling quietly confident when the third man drops his trousers and produces a pathetic example of manhood. However, it just makes 2 inches so the men are set free. Later on, back at camp, the first man says to his companions, "It's a good thing mine was 11 inches."

"It's lucky mine was 9 inches," says the second.

"And it's a bloody good thing I had an erection," answers the third.

A plane crashes in deepest, darkest Africa and there are only five survivors – four men and one woman. It soon becomes obvious that they will never be rescued so they decide to start a small community and make the most of what they have. All goes well for a while except that they all get sexually frustrated and eventually come to an agreement that the woman will spend one week with each man in turn. As it happens, this works very well until three years later the woman falls sick and dies. It turns out to be disastrous for the men. The first week proves difficult, the second awful, the third horrifying and the fourth so impossible that at the beginning of the fifth week, they bury her.

A woman gets onto the train and finds herself sitting opposite a very handsome, sexy man. She smiles at him but gets no reaction. Surprised, she undoes the two top buttons of her blouse revealing more than a little cleavage, hitches up her skirt to show a good deal of thigh but still there is no reaction. By this time, feeling very angry and frustrated, she drops her knickers and straddles his face.
"Aah," smiles the man, "I may be blind but the smell tells me I've arrived at my stop – this must be Grimsby."

Jack was in Paris attending a conference on cabinet making. After the session was finished he decided to have a coffee in one of the many pavement cafés along the Champs-Élysées. He hadn't been there long when a beautiful girl walked by, smiled at him and sat down opposite. Unfortunately she could not speak any English at all, so he took a pen and paper from his briefcase and drew a cup of coffee followed by a question mark. She nodded and he ordered another cup. Later he drew a taxi and again she nodded so they were soon sitting in a cab touring the Left Bank and the sights of Paris. Towards evening he drew a table with wine and food and it wasn't long before they were enjoying a beautiful meal in one of the finest Parisian restaurants. As the meal came to an end, the girl took the pen from Jack and drew a four-poster bed.

"Why, that's amazing," he said. "How on earth did you know I was in the furniture business?"

The train was very crowded as the woman travelled home from work but as she peered through the mass of people she was sure she could see her husband. Pushing her way through the crowds she came up behind him and gave him a lip-smacking kiss on the back of his neck. To her dismay, when he turned round she realised it wasn't her husband.

"Oh, I'm so sorry," she gasped, feeling shocked and confused, "it's just that your head looks like my husband's behind."

It's the 7.55 service from Paddington to Plymouth and a man finds himself sat across the aisle from a beautiful woman. She is reading a large book and as he looks closer at it he realises it's a book on sexual statistics.

"That looks an interesting book," he remarks.

She smiles at him and says, "Yes indeed. There are some fascinating facts here. For instance, it says that on average an Italian has the longest penis and a German has the biggest in diameter. By the way, my name's Sharon, what's yours?"

"Hans Ravellini."

Two parachutists are getting ready to jump and one of them can't help but notice that his companion is wearing dark glasses and holding the lead of a guide dog.

He speaks "May I just say that you have enormous courage to jump when you are blind. I have nothing but the greatest admiration for you. By the way, how do you know when you're near the ground?"

The other replied. "When the lead goes slack."

A Russian couple are walking along the road when a car full of tourists pulls up beside them.

"Excuse me, do you speak English?" asks one of the

passengers in the car.

The couple just look blank and shrug their shoulders.

"Sprechen Sie Deutsch?" they ask. Still no response.

Within the next 30 seconds, the people in the car go through five different languages – French, Italian, Spanish, Chinese and Polish – but still the couple look at them uncomprehending. Eventually the tourists give up and drive away and the Russian woman turns to her companion and remarks, "It must be wonderful to speak so many different languages."

"Rubbish," replies the other. "It didn't get them very far."

It was a foul night and the small boat was sailing perilously close to the rocks. Suddenly the captain shouted to his passengers, "Does anyone know how to pray?"

"Yes, I do," said a pious looking man at the back.

"Okay, you pray and the rest of us will put on life jackets – you see, we're one short."

Due to severe weather conditions some of the scheduled flights had to be cancelled and the passengers found seats on other services. One particular flight to Los Angeles was postponed indefinitely and the ground staff were frantically trying to get the passengers re-booked. As the passengers waited in line, one arrogant man strode to the front of the queue and demanded immediate attention.

"I must have a first-class seat on the next flight," he demanded, "I can't wait here all day."

"Excuse me, Sir, we're going as quickly as we can. If you'd like to get back into the queue we'll see to you as soon as possible," said the airline attendant.

"How dare you dismiss me, young lady!" he spluttered, "Do you know who I am?"

"No, I don't," she said, "but there's no need to panic," and with that, she picked up the microphone and sent out a message over the public address system.

"May I have your attention please. I have a passenger at Gate 11 who does not know who he is. If anyone can help, please come to the gate as soon as you can. Thank you."

A ladies' man stops for the night at a country hotel and as he signs in, he notices a beautiful blonde sitting alone at the hotel bar. While the receptionist is sorting out the paperwork, he saunters over to the blonde and returns a couple of minutes later with the girl on his arm.

Grinning, he says to the receptionist, "Would you believe it! I've just bumped into my wife, so we'd better have a double room."

The following morning, he goes to pay his bill and discovers it's for more than £2,000.

"What the hell's this for?" he splutters. "I've only been here one night."

"Of course, Sir, but your wife has been here for more than a week!"

A man moves to a small town out in the middle of the bush and after a few days he asks the locals what they do for sex. "Shag sheep," comes the reply.

Horrified at the thought, the man ignores them, but two months later with no sign of any female company he eventually gives way and goes out to find himself a little sheep. He takes it back to his place and spends the night in pleasure.

The next morning, feeling much revived, he takes the sheep to the local bar for a drink but when he walks in he's faced with a deadly silence. At last, he can stand it no more and shouts loudly, "What the fuck are you all staring at? It's you lot who told me this is what you do."

"That's right," one of them replies, "but not with the Mayor's special friend."

Travelling through Wales, an Australian tourist spots a farmer with the back legs of a sheep stuck down his wellingtons.

"G'day," says the tourist, "are you shearing that sheep?"

"Not bloody likely," replies the farmer. "Catch one of your own."

Three men find themselves sharing a railway carriage to London.

Two are brothers, the third is a GI soldier.

"Heh! You're American, aren't you?" asks one of the brothers.

"I sure am," he replies. "I'm on leave and I'm going to visit this gal in London."

"What did he say?" asks the other brother, who has very bad hearing problems.

"He says he's going to London to see a girl," shouts the other brother.

"She must be very special for you to come all this way," continues the brother.

"She sure is."

"What's he saying?" asks the deaf brother.

"He says his girl is very special."

"Yep, as soon as she sees me, she rips my clothes off and does things with her little box of tricks that I've only ever dreamed about. My Patsy's a real goer," enthuses the soldier, leaning forwards in his seat.

"What's he saying?" interrupts the deaf brother. "He says he knows our sister," came the reply.

A voluptuous young lady got on the bus but discovered she couldn't climb the stairs because of her tight skirt. She

reached behind her and undid the zipper but it didn't seem to make any difference. So she reached behind her a second time and pulled the zipper down again. All of a sudden, the man standing behind lifted her up and put her on the top step.

"Heh!" she protested. "How dare you!"

"Hold on a minute," he replied. "Once you'd unzipped my fly for the second time, I reckoned we were good friends."

The white missionary had lived in the African village for more than two years. Everything had gone well until one morning, when the Chief sent his men to bring the man before him. He looked at the missionary angrily and said, "Last night, my mother's sister's daughter gave birth to a baby. The baby was white and you are the only white man here. Tonight, you will be tied to that post and burned alive."

After his initial panic, the missionary beckoned the Chief to one side and spoke to him in a low voice.

"Chief, if you look beyond the village, you can see all the sheep grazing on the hill. They are all white except for one black sheep, and there are no other black sheep in the flock. You see what I mean when I say it looks bad."

"Okay, okay," replied the Chief, flustered. "If you don't tell, then I won't tell."

Two couples who had been friends for over 20 years decided to go camping together. On the first night around the campfire they ate and drank well, and were about to retire to their tents when one of the men said, "What do you reckon to all this swapping around then?"

The others got quite enthused about the idea so they decided to try it. A few hours later, one of the men turned to his partner and said, "That was great, I haven't had so much fun in ages, I wonder how the girls got on."

"This lorry is travelling along the motorway when suddenly a car goes past beeping its horn frantically. The lorry driver pulls down his window and shouts, "What's up?"

"You're losing your load."

"You daft prat!" he bellows. "I'm gritting the road."

A couple were driving through remote countryside on a beautiful sunny day when they came across a quaint old pub. They walked into the empty bar and asked the barman what time he opened. "The bar won't be open for another twenty minutes," he said.

"In that case, do you mind if we sit in your garden and wait?" they asked.

"Not at all," he replied. "Would you like a drink while you're waiting?"

LOADS OF MONEY

An upper-class gent was walking through the park when a sudden strong gust of wind blew up the skirt of a passing woman.

"Oh I say, it's airy, isn't it?" he remarked.

The woman replied, "Well what did you expect, feathers?"

The rich and elegant old woman stopped to reverse her Rolls into the only free parking space. But as she was slowly backing in, a young girl in a nifty little sports car came up behind her and nipped into the space.

"You've got to be young and daring to do that," laughed the girl.

The old woman ignored her and continued to reverse into the parking spot, slowly crunching the sports car underneath the Rolls' wheels. When she had finished she turned to the dumbfounded girl and said, "You've got to be old and rich to do that."

The rich boyfriend presented his girlfriend with a beautiful fur coat made out of skunk.

"I'm amazed", she said, "that such a gorgeous coat could

come from such a stinking little beast."

"Well, fuck off," said the boyfriend. "I didn't expect much gratitude but there's no need to get so personal."

A woman has her portrait painted by a local artist and asks him if he would paint her dripping with fabulous jewels. She explains, "If I die before my husband and he gets married again, I want his second wife to go crazy looking for the stones."

A very rich couple buy a mansion and 20 acres of land in the country and hire three maids, two man-servants and a gardener to take care of themselves and the upkeep of the property. Now the lady of the house likes her grog and after one particularly heavy night on the booze, the next morning she decides to take a walk around the grounds to clear her head. She bumps into the young gardener and after passing the time of day with him, she mentions her hangover.

"I can't even remember going to bed," she tells him.

"Begging your pardon, Ma'am, but I put you to bed when I saw you had fallen asleep on the patio. I hung your dress up so that it would not be spoiled."

"But John, when I woke up this morning I was naked."

"Begging your pardon, Ma'am. I took off your bra and pants because I thought they might be uncomfortable."

The woman blushes and laughs nervously.
"Good gracious, John, I must have been tight."
"Not after the first time, Ma'am."

Three brothers are left their father's business in his will. The oldest son says, "Dad left me 48% of the shares so I'm going to be Chairman."

"OK," says the second son, "and I'll be in charge of the everyday running of the business because I've got 30% of the shares."

"Now wait a minute," says the third and youngest son. "What about me, don't forget I've got 22% of the shares?"

The other two confer amongst themselves and then reply, "We've decided you can be in charge of sexual matters."

"What does that mean?"

"When we want your fucking advice, we'll ask for it."

"Hello, Bates," said Lady Symthe to the gardener. "Do you think you're a good sport?"

"I believe so, yes Ma'am," replied the puzzled man.

"And do you think you're a good fuck?" she asked, unbuttoning her blouse to reveal nothing on underneath.

"I think I am, yes," stammered the blushing gardener.

"Well, if that's so, fuck off, it's April Fools Day."

The Chairman turned to his secretary and said, "I'll never forget that weekend we spent together in the country, will you?"
"I don't know," she replied, "it depends how much it's worth."

There had been an awful car accident resulting in a flashy sports car hitting a roadside tree and badly injuring the two passengers. When the emergency services arrived, the man was screaming hysterically.
"Try and calm down, Sir," said the paramedic, "and we'll try and see what's wrong. At least you weren't flung through the windscreen like your girlfriend."
"Aagh!" screamed the man even more, "Have you not seen what she has in her mouth?"

The poor man was in great difficulties. His business was failing and it looked as if he was facing bankruptcy. As a last resort he popped into the local church and kneeling down he prayed fervently.
"Oh God, please don't let this happen to me, please let me win the lottery."
But on Saturday night, he had no luck. The following week,

the situation got worse. The man lost his house and all his possessions, so once again he went into church and prayed desperately.

"Oh please, please I beg you, please let me win the lottery."

But on Saturday, he had no luck. On the following Monday, his wife and children left him and he was now completely on his own. He ran into church, got down on his knees and pleaded, "Oh God, everything has gone, I have nothing left. Have pity on me, I beg you. Why won't you help me win the lottery?"

At that moment, there was a tremendous thunderclap, a bright flashing light and God boomed out, "You daft bugger, you could at least give yourself a sporting chance and buy a fucking ticket!"

The retired colonel is striding out through the village when he is accosted by one of his manservants who's a little the worse for wear.

"Hello, your colonel sir," grins the man. "How the devil are we?" he mimics.

Not only drunk but insulting, the colonel is outraged and remarks forcefully, "Drunk as a skunk!"

The man whispers conspirationally, "Don't worry, Sir, your secret's safe with me, I've had a bit to drink myself."

Lady Cynthia, a spinster for 60 years, was finally forced to get married because of financial difficulties within her aristocratic family. On the night of the honeymoon, she walked into the bedroom wearing a long white nightdress and a pair of long white gloves.

"What's this for, old girl?" demanded her new husband. "Why are you wearing gloves?"

She replied haughtily, "One has been informed that one has to actually handle the so-called member."

"Oh Jasmin, was it love at first sight?"

"No, second. I didn't know he had so much money the first time."

Two men are crossing the Pennines when their car packs up on them and they are left stranded. Fortunately, they spot a little cottage and decide to ask for shelter. The door is opened by a widow who immediately invites them in and gives them something to eat.

"I'm sorry, I only have a single bed in the spare room, so one of you will have to share with me. Steve picks the short straw and ends up sleeping with the widow who is so starved for sex that the night turns out to be very passionate.

The following morning, they have breakfast and say goodbye.

"Martin, I've got something to confess," says Steve. "When she asked me for my name and address I gave her yours. You know what my wife is like, she'd have murdered me."

However, Martin is not amused and when they return home, they don't see each other for over a year, until they meet up again in the bank.

"I'm glad I've seen you," says Martin. "I've had a letter from the solicitor of that widow, he…"

But before he can continue, Steve interrupts.

"Listen, I really am sorry about that. As it happens, my wife's left me anyway."

"No, no," says Martin. "I just wanted to let you know that the widow has died and left me £2 million."

The church was in a very bad state of repair and all sorts of fundraising ideas were being considered. It was decided that some of the wealthy business people could be approached and on this morning, the vicar was escorting a local millionaire around the church to see for himself the critical state it was in. As the vicar pointed out the cracks in the stonework over the front porch, a piece of masonry fell off and hit the millionaire on the head. Rubbing his head gingerly, the man said, "I see what you mean, Vicar, here's a cheque for £200."

As they were leaving, the vicar looked up and shouted, "Go on, Lord, hit the tight-fisted bugger again!"

Two old school chums who haven't seen each other for twenty years bump into each other in the local supermarket.

"Hello, Tara, how are you?" asks Helen.

"Very well," replies Tara, who's an awful show-off. "Very well indeed. After I left school, I went into my father's business in Switzerland and some years later, I married the son of one of Switzerland's largest chocolate manufacturers.

"Oh how nice," says Helen.

"And then we returned to England some years ago, where we started an exclusive health farm, catering mostly for the local celebrities. It's been a huge success."

"Oh how nice," says Helen.

"And now we're branching out into our own range of cosmetics, and they are proving to be very popular."

"Oh how nice," says Helen.

"Anyway, that's enough of me. How about you, Helen?"

"Me? Well I went on to finishing school, where one of the most important things they taught me was to say, 'Oh, how nice' instead of 'Fuck you."

"Come in," said the bank manager to his customer, "and what can I do for you?"

The customer explained that he was an inventor and he needed some funding for his latest invention. He had created a special substance that, sprayed lightly over a woman's pussy, would give it a strawberry flavour.

"No, no," said the banker, shaking his head sadly. "That's no good, but if you could invest a substance that, sprayed on a strawberry, would make it taste like pussy, then you're onto a winner and I'd buy into the company myself."

"Now listen very carefully," said the millionaire to the architect designing his new house. **"Whatever you do, I don't want that tree disturbed over there. It brings back fond memories."**

"Why's that?" asked the architect.

"That's where I had sex for the first time. And don't touch that old tree over there either. That's where her mother was standing and that's where she watched us while we were doing it."

"What?" said the architect. **"You were shagging her daughter and she was watching! What did she say?"**

"Baaaa."

SHOPPING SPREE

A Scotsman, a bit the worse for wear, staggered into an off licence for some more booze. There were two men in front of him. The first had a huge beard and a big cigar. He ordered £100 worth of spirits and told the shop assistant to put it on the F11 convention bill. After he had gone the second man, also sporting a large cigar and a slightly smaller beard, ordered £200 of sherry and port, and asked for it to be also put on the F11 convention account. So the Scotsman thought he'd try and get away with the same thing.

"Two crates of whisky please, and put it on the F11 convention account, my good man," he said, trying to sound very upright and sober. The shop assistant replied, "I'm sorry, Sir, I can't do that, you don't have a large beard and cigar."

For a moment the Scotsman looked defeated but then a smile lit up his face as he lifted his kilt and replied, "Ah yes, but I'm working undercover."

A sleazy man ran a pet shop and advertised on the front window that he had a dog for sale, specially reared for spinsters.

It wasn't long before a woman came in asking for more details.

"I assure you, Miss, this dog will cater for all your needs," he said as he brought out a huge Alsatian for her to inspect. The woman bought the dog and they went home. However, a week later, he received an angry phone call from her, complaining that the dog was not satisfactory.

"My sincere apologies," simpered the man. "I'll come round and see you straight away."

When the man arrived, he found the woman in bed and the dog asleep on the carpet.

"Watch carefully, Brutus," he said to the dog as he took his clothes off. "I'm only going to show you one more time."

The man knocked on his manager's door.

"Excuse me, Sir, may I have tomorrow off, the wife wants to go shopping."

"Certainly not," replied the manager.

"Oh thank you, Sir, you've saved my life!"

A man was strolling around an old antique market when he spotted a long-forgotten brass rat pushed into a far corner of one of the shops. A collector of brass objects, the purchase was soon made and the man departed. However, he hadn't gone too far when he noticed a rat running up behind him and within minutes, the whole area was swimming in the vermin. Frightened for his life, the man raced down the road to the river and threw the brass rat into the water. Lo and behold all the rats ran into the water and drowned. Some time later, he returned to the antique market and sought out the man who had sold him the rat. When the shopkeeper recognised him, he said, "Back again already, Sir, is there something wrong with your figure?"

"Oh no, not at all, I was just wondering if you had any brass figures of lawyers," he replied.

A bloke goes into a baker's and asks for three pork pies. The assistant picks the pies up with a pair of tongs and puts them in a paper bag. The man then asks for three strawberry tarts and the assistant picks up another pair of tongs and puts three tarts into a bag.

"I must compliment you on such impressive hygienic standards," said the man.

"Thank you," says the assistant. "We're very careful not to touch any of the food."

Just as the man is leaving the shop, he notices a piece of string hanging from the assistant's trousers.

"Excuse me, what is that piece of string?" he asks.

"That's used when I go to the toilet. So that I don't touch my penis. I pull it out with the string," says the assistant.

"But how do you put it back?"

"Oh, I use one of these pairs of tongs."

The couple had been married many years and it had got to the stage where any romance that might have been, had died long ago. On a shopping trip into town they stopped off at the tailor's to get the husband fitted for a new pair of trousers.

"What size zip would you like?" asked the assistant.

"Oh, the longest you've got," he quickly replied.

After they'd left the shop the wife turned to him and remarked bitterly, "You remind me of that good-for-nothing brother of yours. Every day he opens the doors of his double garage and wheels out a bicycle."

A very shy man had the embarrassing task of returning a pair of underpants to the shop and being served by a pretty young girl.

"What's wrong with them, Sir?" she asked.

"They're, they're ... er, unsatisfactory," he said, blushing madly.

"Can you tell me why?"

The man was lost for words but as he was looking wildly around for inspiration, an idea came to him.

"Do you know the old Grand Hotel on Union Street?"

"Yes."

"And do you know the ballroom underneath?"

"But there is no ballroom underneath."

"Exactly!" exclaimed the man, "and that's just what's wrong with these underpants."

A woman tries on an evening dress in the shop and says to the sales assistant, "What do you think, I know the neckline's a bit low cut, is it too daring?"

"Well, Madam, have you got hairs on your chest?" said the assistant.

"No."

"Then I think it's too daring."

"There you are, does it fit properly?" he asked.

"Oh yes, it's great," she replied.

"It doesn't hurt, does it?"

"Not at all."

"Well, that's good, because we've only got these shoes in this size."

There was only one supermarket basket left at the door of the shop as a woman and a man approached from separate directions.

"Excuse me," said the woman, "do you want that basket?"

"No thanks," he replied, "I'm only after one thing."

"Typical male," she said to herself as he walked away.

Coming home from work, a man passed a sex shop and on impulse went in and bought a blow-up doll. He couldn't wait to get home to try it out but when he pumped her up, she just went flat again. The next day the man went back to the sex shop and demanded to see the manager.

"So what exactly was wrong with the doll?" he asked.

"I'll tell you what," he replied angrily. "As soon as I'd blown her up, she went down on me."

"Bloody hell," exclaimed the manager. "If I'd known that I'd have charged you twice as much!"

The man was approached by the most beautiful sales girl he had ever seen.

"Can I help you, Sir," she said. "What would you like?"

"What would I like...?" he mused. "I would like to take you away from all this. We would go to the most elegant restaurant in town, linger over the port and then head back to my place for soft lights, sweet music and mad passionate love."

He sighed, "That's what I'd like, but what I need is a new shirt."

A gay man walked into a sex shop and pointed to a large black penis behind the counter.

"I'll have that one please," he said.

"OK, sir, shall I wrap it up or just put it in a bag?"
"Neither," replied the man, "I'll just eat it right now."

A woman went into a sex shop and asked the assistant for a vibrator.
Wagging his finger at her, he said, "Come this way."
She replied, "If I could come that way, I wouldn't need a vibrator."

SMALL TALK

The little boy's mother had been away for a week's conference and on returning she asked her son how he'd been.

"OK," said Ben. "Except there was dreadful thunder and lightning on Tuesday night so me and Daddy snuggled up in the same bed."

"You mean Daddy and I," said his young nanny.

"Oh no," said the boy, "that was Wednesday night, don't you remember?"

When Samantha was expecting twins she interrupted a burglary and got shot twice in the stomach. Fortunately, the babies were delivered safely but the bullets were never recovered. Seventeen years went by, when one day her daughter came to her in great distress.

"Oh mum, I just been to do a wee and all of a sudden, out popped a bullet."

Samantha told her it was nothing to worry about and explained what had happened all those years ago. A little later she caught sight of her son, sitting down with his head in his hands. She went up to him, put her arms round his shoulders and said, "Don't worry, I think I can guess what happened. You went to the toilet and a bullet came out."

"Oh no, mum, it wasn't like that. I was having a wank and I shot the dog."

It was an idyllic scene. Little old Grandma was sitting in her rocking chair, knitting a jumper for her granddaughter. On the floor in front of her chair sat her two beautiful grandchildren, quietly looking at some picture books. All of a sudden, the children turned to Grandma, saying, "Oh Grandma, please tell us a story. We love your stories, please, please!"

"Well … I don't know," replied Grandma. "I'm a bit tired."

"Oh please, Grandma, tell us our favourite story about when you were a whore in Liverpool."

As the young girl leaves school for home, a car draws up and a man leans across, saying, "Hello, let me give you a lift home."

"No thanks," she says firmly and heads on up the road.

The car follows and again the man speaks to her.

"Come on, get in, I've bought you a comic."

"No, I don't want to," she cries and starts to run.

The car catches her up again and the man says, "Look, it's starting to rain, you're going to get so wet if you don't get in."

"How many times do I have to say no?" she screams. "It was

your choice to buy the Lada but it doesn't mean I have to ride in it, Dad."

"Grandpa, have you got your own football?" asked his grandson. Puzzled, Grandpa replied, "No, Billy, I don't play football anymore, why do you ask?"
"Because I heard Dad say that when you kicked it, we'd all be able to afford a good holiday."

During Sunday school, Tracy turned to her teacher and said, "Please Miss, I've found out where God lives."
"Really!" smiled the teacher. "Where does he live?"
"At number 12 Beech Street."
"How do you know that?"
"Yesterday, I was passing it on the way to school and I heard a woman from the upstairs bedroom shouting "Oh God, Oh God…"

A little boy ran into his mother's room crying hysterically.
"I don't want my willy any more," he sobbed, "it's bad to have one."
"Don't be silly, darling," she replied. "Of course it's not bad, why do you say that?"

"Because I've just seen daddy in the bathroom and he's trying to pull his off."

"Daddy, daddy," cried little Tom, "please come and look, my pussy cat is lying in the garden with his feet in the air and he won't move."

Assuming the worst, dad went into the garden to take a look.

"I'm sorry, son, I'm afraid Tiddles is dead."

Through his sobs, the little boy asked why the cat's feet were sticking up in the air.

Quick as a flash, dad replied, "That's so Jesus can grab hold of them and take him up to heaven."

A few days later, dad came home from work to find Tom crying in the garden.

"What's happened, Tom?" he asked.

"It's mummy, she nearly died today, like my poor pussy cat!"

"How can that be?" asked dad aghast.

"I went into the summer house a little while back and mummy was there with her feet in the air shouting 'I'm coming, I'm coming!' Oh daddy, if it hadn't been for the milkman holding her down, she would have been taken up to heaven by Jesus."

★ ★ ★

A little boy went shopping with his mother and when she began trying some clothes on in the fitting room, he remarked, "You've got big balloons, mum."

"That's not the right word for them" she replied. "Why do you call them that?"

"Because yesterday I saw daddy blowing up the au pair's."

Mrs Primly is walking down the village street when she sees young Emily pulling a cow by a rope.

"Goodness me," she utters. "What on earth are you doing with that?"

"I'm taking it to the bull," she replies.

"The bull! What a thing to ask a young girl, can't your dad do it?"

"Oh no," replies the girl, "it has to be the bull."

A family went on holiday to the coast and wandered accidentally onto a nudist beach. The little boy ran off to play but returned a few minutes later, saying, "Mummy, mummy, I've just seen some women with boobs much much bigger than yours."

Mummy replied, "Son, the bigger they are, the more stupid the women."

The little boy went off again but soon came running back.

"Mummy, mummy, I've just seen some men with much bigger willies than daddy has."

As before, mummy replied, "The bigger they are, the more

stupid the men."

Five minutes went past and the little boy came back very excited. "Mummy, mummy, I've just seen daddy talking to the most stupid lady I've ever seen, and as he was talking to her, he started to get more and more stupid as well."

"Daddy," said the serious little girl. "May I have a computer for Christmas please?"

"I'm sorry, darling, not at the moment, your mum and I have a pile of heavy bills and our new car is costing us heaps of money each month."

The following spring, the little girl asked her father again for a computer but he repeated what he had told her before. A week later, early in the morning, daddy saw his daughter leaving the house with a suitcase in her hand.

"Where are you going?" he asked.

"I'm leaving," said the little girl. "Last night I was walking past your room when I heard you telling Mum you were pulling out and I heard her telling you to wait because she was coming too. So there's no way I'm staying here to cope with all the bills."

Down the street, a young girl walked into her parents' bedroom to find her mother astride her father. To cover any embarrassment they told her they were playing a game.

"Can I join in?" she asked.

"Of course."

So the girl sits astride dad as well, jumping up and down, pretending dad is a horse. As the parents reach a climax, the little girl shouts excitedly, "Hold on tight, Mum, this is where me and the au pair usually fall off!"

Did you hear about the couple who adopted a baby from Spain? Then signed up for evening classes in Spanish so that they would be able to understand the baby when it started talking.

A priest met a small boy walking along the street and in the boy's hand was a bottle of acid.

"Now, now young man," said the priest, looking worried. "That's not something you should be walking around with. Look, wouldn't you rather have some of my Holy Water?"

"Why?" asked the boy. "What does that do?"

"Well, only this morning I put this water on Mrs McTavish's tummy and she passed a baby."

"Not bad," said the boy, "but five minutes ago, I put this acid on the backside of that old black and white mongrel and it passed the police car."

"Okay darling," said Mummy to her little five-year-old daughter. "Why don't you say grace for us today?"

"Yes Mummy," replied the dutiful daughter. She closed her eyes, put her hands together and said innocently, "Give us some food, for Christ's sake. Amen."

"Mummy, Mummy, where do babies come from?" asked the little girl.

"Why darling, they come from the storks."

"But Mummy, who fucks the storks?"

MALE MENOPAUSE

It was a series of subtle signs that told Johnny Sharpe he was in a mid-life crisis and about to dive into the male menopause. When filling in forms under "age" he put 49? and under sex "only very occasionally". It now took him all night to do what he used to do all night. He found it strange, fancying a red Porsche, when he'd never ever driven. Eventually he went to the doctor and said he felt useless, finished, incompetent and ignored. The doctor simply said "Next," before prescribing that he have an operation to dampen down his ambition and then have some whore-moan replacement therapy at the local brothel.

PLAYING AWAY

A man went to the doctor's complaining that his wife had such a vigorous sex drive that she was wearing him out. The doctor suggested he bring his wife into the surgery for an examination, so they both turned up the following week.

The wife was told to go into the other room and strip off, but when the doctor went in, he was overcome by her beautiful body and the way she started to tempt him over.

"It's no good, I can't help myself," gasped the doctor and he stripped off frantically and jumped on top of her.

After some time, the groans of pleasure attracted the husband's attention so he opened the door to see what was going on.

"What the hell do you think you're doing?" bellowed the husband.

"I'm, er…, taking her temperature," replied the flustered doctor.

Taking a gun out of his pocket, the man said, "When you take that thing out, it better have numbers on it then."

A tall dark handsome man pops into the vet's and asks the receptionist how long he will have to wait.

"Oh, about 30 minutes, Mr Wellbeing has two cats and a gerbil to see."

"Thank you," replies the man and walks out. Over the next

few weeks the man appears several times, asks the same question and then leaves. By this time, the receptionist is so intrigued, she tells the vet and he suggests that next time the man comes in she should follow him when he leaves.

So the receptionist does as she's asked and on returning says to the vet, "Well, that's very strange. All he seems to do is go straight round to your house."

"How do you like my new suit?" said Steve to his friend.

"Wow! That must have cost a lot of money?"

"I don't know, it was a present from my wife. When I arrived home early yesterday afternoon, it was hanging over the bottom of the bed."

"Jane, that milkman will have to go," said the enraged husband. "He's so cheeky, he reckons he's slept with every woman on this street, except one."

"Oh, I know who that'll be," replied his wife, "It'll be her at No. 32."

"I'm sorry to hear your Dave's in hospital, I heard it was his knee."

"That's right, I found a blonde sitting on it."

The man was so angry when he found his wife in bed with another man that he punched him unconscious and took him downstairs and out into the garden shed. When the man came round he found his penis was chained to the ground and beside it was a large knife.

"What are you going to do?" he stammered.

"I'm not going to do anything," smirked the husband, "but you might want to chop it off to escape the flames when I set fire to this shed."

Jack had not long left for work when he realised he'd left some important papers at home, so he drove back and on entering the kitchen, found his wife bending over the cooker. Quick as a flash, he lifted her skirt and unzipped his flies, just as she said without turning round, "Hello, Fred, you're early this week."

The phone rings and the husband answers it.

"No, mate, you want the Met Office."

"Who was that, darling?" asks the wife.

"I don't know, I think he wanted the weather forecast, because he asked me if the coast was clear."

A man went to the doctor's in an awful state. Cuts and bruises to his face and a suspected broken arm.

"What happened to you?" asked the doctor.

"It's my wife, she had one of her dreadful nightmares."

"Do you mean she did this to you while she was asleep?"

"Oh no, doctor, it was when she shouted out in her sleep, 'Quick, get out, my husband's coming home,' that, without thinking, I jumped out of the window."

"You never make a noise or cry out when you have an orgasm," he complained.

"How would you know, you're never there," she retorted.

Following a night of fantastic sex with a woman he picked up in the pub, the man is afraid to go home and face his wife.

"I have a great idea," says the woman. "Stick these darts in your back pocket and tell her the truth. Trust me, it will be alright."

So, with trepidation, the man returns home to find his wife in the kitchen waiting for him.

"Okay," she hisses, "where the hell have you been this time?"

"I've been making wonderful love to a beautiful woman, all night long," he replies.

"You bloody liar, pull the other one. You've been with your mates playing darts, I can see them in your back pocket."

"What the hell's going on here?" yelled the angry husband, on finding his wife and the gardener canoodling in the summer house."
"You see," said the wife scornfully, "I told you he was stupid."

Two men were chatting over the garden wall. The first said, "You'll never guess what happened this morning, Tom. My wife was suffering from a hangover, so I went downstairs to make her a cup of tea. Because it was cold, I grabbed the first thing I saw to put on which turned out to be her dressing gown. I was just bending over the fridge to get the milk, when the window cleaner walked in, put his hand up me and grabbed my bum. You can imagine the embarrassment when he realised who I was, it was just an astonishing coincidence that his wife had a dressing gown exactly the same."

Samantha had been staying with her sick mother for over a month and on returning home, she discovered her husband had been having an affair. She confronted him, shouting

325

loudly, "Was it Jane, from next door?"

"No."

"Was it Emma?"

"No."

"Then it must have been Kate."

"No, you stupid woman. Don't you think I have any friends of my own?"

The angry woman marched round to her next door neighbour's house and confronted her with a set of photographs.

"Look at these, you common tart, this is proof that you've been seeing my husband. There's one of the two of you in bed, this is a picture of you and him in the back seat of the car and this one shows you sitting on his knee. What do you have to say for yourself?" she snarled.

For a few moments, the next-door neighbour looked through the photographs and then said, "Mmm, not bad. I'll have two copies of the first picture and one each of the other two."

It was the same routine every night. Fred would arrive home from the coal mine and jump into the bath that his wife always had ready for him, and then she would lovingly wash his back. However, one evening it all changed. When Fred

got into the bath, his wife took a brush to him and scrubbed
him till he was red raw.

"Hey, woman," he yelled. "What's going on?"

"You tell me," she retorted. "For as long as I can remember
you've always walked into the house dead on 6 o'clock, black
from head to toe. But tonight, you're 45 minutes late and a
small part of you is white."

Old Joe only had moments to live. At his bedside were his
family – his wife and four sons, three of whom had blond
hair, the other had ginger.

"Em, tell me please, I've always wondered why one of our
sons had red hair. Is he really my son?"

Emma put her hand on her heart and swore fervently that,
yes, he was his son.

"Oh thank goodness," croaked the old man and he died with
a smile on his face.

As the family left the room, the wife sighed deeply.

"Thank heaven he didn't ask about the other three."

A man takes the afternoon off work and comes home
unexpectedly to find his wife lying on the bed, naked and
out of breath.

"What's going on?" he asks.

"I think I'm having an asthma attack," she gasps.

He rushes to the phone to ring for a doctor when his son runs in.

"Daddy, daddy, Uncle Bill is in the wardrobe and he's got no clothes on."

"What!" shouts the man, and back up the stairs he rushes to find his brother hiding naked in the wardrobe.

"Why, you bloody prat," he shouts angrily, "there's my wife having a severe asthma attack and all you can do is play hide and seek and scare the kids!"

A man went to an old furniture shop to buy an antique kitchen table. Almost at once, he saw the table he wanted to buy and asked the price.

"£2,000 sir."

"Never!" exclaimed the man, "That's unbelievably expensive."

"That's true," replied the assistant, but this is not just any antique kitchen table, this piece of furniture has special powers."

"Get away! Show me."

The assistant went up to the table and said, "How many floors are there in this building?"

Immediately, the table jumped into the air four times, and indeed there were four floors in the building.

The man wasn't totally convinced.

"OK, ask it how much money I've got in my wallet."

The question was asked and the table jumped up and down

eleven times.

"That's incredible," said the man. "It's true, I've got two £5 notes and a loose £1 coin. I must have that table."

So the man paid £2,000 and the antique kitchen table was delivered the next day. While it was being installed, his mate popped over and remarked on the piece of new purchase.

"It's very special," said the man. "Here, I'll show you." He thought for a moment and then said, "How much money has my wife got in her bank account?"

The table went completely berserk. It started jumping up and down and was still going 30 minutes later.

"But how can that be? Where did she get all that money?" he said, flabbergasted.

Suddenly, the table stopped moving, its legs fell apart and its drawers fell to the floor.

"Doctor, doctor, I'm having trouble with my todger, can you do anything for me?" said the distressed man.

After a thorough examination the doctor told him that he must have been so sexually active in the past that he'd almost worn it out. The fact is that he'd only got the use of it for another 25 shags. The young man went home to his wife and told her what the doctor had said.

"Oh no!" she cried, "We mustn't waste any of them, we'll have to draw up a carefully planned timetable."

"I've already done that," he said, "on the way home, and there isn't a slot left for you."

★ ★ ★

The couple had been married a year when the husband was called away on business on the other side of the country. It would mean he would be away for a month so the wife's friend moved in to keep her company. As it happened, the job finished earlier than expected so he jumped on a plane and on landing rang his wife from the airport. Her friend answered the phone to say that Tracy was in the bath.

"OK, can you tell her I'll be there about midnight so if she can wear something sheer and sexy we'll make it a night to remember."

"OK," said the friend, "and who shall I say called?"

The old farmer married a young girl of 18 and after a few months of idyllic married life, he went to see his doctor.

"The problem is I'm having to work many hours on the farm but I have to keep breaking off when I get the urge, to run back to the house, jump into bed and do the business. Then it's back to work, and it's knackering me."

The doctor suggested that his wife should come to see him out in the fields.

"Every time you get the urge," said the doctor, "fire a shot from your gun to let your wife know you're waiting for her. A few months passed and then the doctor met the old farmer in the high street.

"How's the shotgun plan working?" he asked.

"Oh it was very good at first, but then the duck shooting season started and I haven't seen her since," he replied sadly.

The man rang his wife to tell her he had the afternoon off and would be coming home. The phone was answered by a small boy.

"Hello son, can I speak to mum?"

"No," said the boy, "mum's in bed with the milkman and they've told me to stay downstairs."

The man was stunned by the news but after a moment or two he said to the boy, "Son, go and get my shotgun from the garage, load it with two bullets and go and blast them."

After an agonising 10 minutes the little boy came back onto the phone.

"I've done it, dad," he said.

"Well done, son, I'll finish off when I get back. Go and have a swim in the pool to clean yourself up and I'll see you later."

"But dad, we don't have a pool," said the boy.

"What! Hold on, is that 0397 46461?"

After months of trying, the Office Manager finally managed to persuade his beautiful secretary to come out to dinner with him. Afterwards they went back to her flat and after some coffee and a little foreplay, they jumped into bed. Alas,

no matter how hard he tried, he could not get an erection and full of apologies and acute embarrassment, he went home. He got into bed next to his big, fat ugly wife who was snoring her head off and as his body touched her naked flesh, he got a huge erection. Jumping out of bed he looked down at his swollen organ and said sadly, "Now I know why they call you a prick."

A man comes home early from work to find his wife in bed with another man.
"Who the bloody hell is this?" he shouts angrily.
"Good question," she replies. "Say, lover, what's your name?"

A man came home early from work to find his wife in bed with another man. The man's head was lying between the wife's voluptuous breasts.
"What the bloody hell are you doing?" shouted the husband.
"Listening to some good music," replied the man calmly.
"Get off, let me hear", but when the husband put his head between her breasts he couldn't hear anything.
"Of course not," replied the man arrogantly. "You're not plugged in."

A woman was in bed with her lover when she heard her husband open the front door.

"Quick!" she whispered urgently, "It's my husband, hide in the wardrobe."

"Ooh, it's dark in here," said a little voice.

"Who's that?" gasped the man.

"That's my mum you've been with and I'm going to call my dad."

"Now, now, son, not so hasty. I'm sure we can work this out."

"OK," said the small boy. "But it's going to cost you."

"How about £5?"

"I'm going to call dad."

"Well, £10 then."

"I'm going to call dad."

"OK, let's say £20."

"No, £30."

"Well, that's all I've got, here you are." The man handed over the money and made his escape when the coast was clear.

A few days later mum took the little boy to church and as she knelt to pray he wandered off and crept into the confessional.

"Ooh, it's dark in here," he said.

"Oh no, don't start that again," replied the agitated priest.

The little boy's mum had shaved off all her pubic hair, ready to wear her skimpy bikini when they went on holiday.
"Where's all your hair gone?" asked her son.

"I've lost my sponge," she replied dismissively and told him to go out to play. Sometime later he returned with a big smile on his face.

"Mummy, mummy, am I a good boy for finding your sponge?"

Puzzled, mum asked him where it was and he answered her proudly, "The lady across the road is washing daddy's face with it."

Saturday morning was the time for all the milk accounts to be settled and the task of collecting the money fell to a young man who accompanied the milkman. Number 47 Lansdowne Road was opened by a bored and lonely woman who suggested that instead of paying the £6 bill, she might pay him in sex. The young man agreed, stepped inside and they went into a back room. As she removed her clothes, he dropped his trousers to reveal the biggest todger she'd ever seen. But as she watched, he took a number of washers out of his pocket and slipped them over his massive hardware.

"You don't have to do that," she said, "I can take anything you can give me."

"Maybe," he replied, "but not for a small bill of just £6."

The man came home early from work to find his wife lying naked on the bed, crying her eyes out.

"What's wrong?" he asked.

"I've got nothing to wear to the dance tomorrow night," she sobbed.

"Oh come on now! You've plenty of clothes," and with that he went over to the wardrobe. "See here, there's the nice pink dress, the pale blue skirt, the yellow cocktail dress, hi there Tom, the green silk gown..."

The simple man was beside himself with anger when he discovered his wife in bed with another man.

"How could you?" he yelled, and taking a gun out of the bottom drawer of the bedside table he placed it to his head and cocked the trigger.

"Don't Jim, please don't," sobbed the woman, "put the gun down."

Jim replied angrily, "Shut up and start saying your prayers, you're next."

Two men were talking over the garden fence when the fire station's alarm went off. Immediately, Jack bid his mate goodbye and headed for the gate.

"Heh Jack," his mate shouted out to him, "how long have you been a volunteer fireman?"

"I'm not," replied Jack, "but my lover's husband is."

King John was off to the crusades, but before he left, he told his faithful servant that he would leave with him the key of his wife's chastity belt for safe keeping.

"If you don't hear from me within five years, you can let her out," he said.

The King set off, but he'd only been gone an hour when his trusty servant caught up with him.

"Sire, Sire," he panted. "You gave me the wrong key!"

An old man was very sad because he had mislaid his favourite hat, so on impulse, he decided to steal one from the church vestibule when morning service was on. Unfortunately, the verger walked in just as he was about to commit the deadly deed, so he was forced to attend the service. Later, as he came out, he stopped to talk to the vicar.

"Thank you very much for that wonderful sermon on the ten commandments. I had intended to steal a hat but after listening to what you had to say, I decided against it."

"Well, that makes my job worthwhile," beamed the vicar. "I suppose it was the commandment 'Thou shalt not steal' which stopped you stealing the hat?"

"Oh no, vicar. It was the one which said 'Thou shalt not commit adultery'. As soon as you mentioned it, I remembered where I had left my hat."

A man returned home early from work to discover his wife in bed with a naked man. "How dare you!" he bellowed. "Come here you bastard, I'll teach you a lesson you won't forget."

"Now wait a minute, Tom," interrupted his wife. "You remember that new car I got last spring? Well, he gave it to me. And that smashing holiday we went on, well, he paid for that. And I think we could do with a new roof on the house soon."

"Whatever are you thinking of?" replied the husband. "He'll get cold if you don't cover him up, and I'm sure he could do with a nice cup of tea."

SMART REMARKS

Did you hear about the two cannibals who caught a clown? As they began eating it, one said to the other, "Hey, wait a minute, do you taste something funny?"

Why do Scotsmen wear kilts?
So the sheep won't hear the zip.

A bad football team is like an old bra.
No cups and very little support.

What have a diamond ring and David Beckham got in common?
Both come in a posh box.

What do you say to a woman with no arms and no legs?
Nice tits, sweetheart.

What do you call a woman who always knows where her husband is?
A widow.

What's the difference between a cockerel and a nymphomaniac?
The cockerel says "Cock-a-doodle-do" while the nymphomaniac cries "Any cock'll do!"

What does a woman have when she's got two little balls in her hand?
The man's undivided attention.

Why are men more clever than dogs?
So they won't hump women's legs at dinner parties.

What's the definition of female masturbation?
Finishing the job off properly.

Why is it so difficult for women to find caring, sensitive men?
They already have boyfriends.

What's the difference between an egg and a wank?
You can beat an egg.

What's the difference between a woman and a fast food chicken take-away?
Once you've had the breast and leg all that's left is a greasy box to stick your bone in.

What's the definition of a yankee?
It's like a quickie, only you can do it yourself.

What's the difference between like and love?
Spit and swallow.

A dangerous lunatic escaped from the mental institution and raped a laundry woman before making his escape.
The headline in the local paper read, "Nut screws washer and bolts."

Old saying: "Fighting for peace is like fucking for virginity."

What's the difference between a vulture and your mother-in-law?
A vulture waits until you're dead.

Why do firemen have bigger balls than policemen?
They sell more tickets.

How many men does it take to change a roll of toilet paper?
No one knows, it's never happened.

Did you hear about the nymphomaniac who robbed a bank?
She tied up the safe and blew the guard.

Old proverb:
Girls who look for trouble often get a belly full.

Is it true that if mini skirts get any shorter, women will have two more lips to paint, two more cheeks to powder, and a little more hair to comb?

Wise old saying:
Girls who use their heads can stop the population explosion.

Words of wisdom from a philosopher:
"It all comes down to the same thing in the end. Live life like a dog. If you can't eat it or fuck it, then piss on it."

Old saying:
May your organ never quit while you are halfway through your favourite piece.

A bloke walked into the pub and was astounded at the sight of the barman. He was built like a brick shithouse with muscles bulging out all over, tattoos everywhere, unshaven and sweaty.

After a moment or two the barman became aware of the looks he was getting and said, "What the bloody hell are you looking at?"

"Sorry, mate, it's just that you look just like someone I know. You're almost identical…if it wasn't for the moustache…"

"But I haven't got a moustache," said the barman.

"No, but my wife has."

What's the difference between a penis and a bonus?
Your wife will always blow your bonus.

What's the smartest thing ever to come out of a woman's mouth?
Einstein's dick.

Why do women rub their eyes in the morning?
Because they don't have bollocks.

Why are wives like condoms?
They both spend too much time in your wallet and not enough time on the end of your dick.

What's the difference between a battery and a woman?
A battery has a positive side.

What's the first thing a nymphomaniac learns when she starts taking driving lessons?
You can also sit up in a car.

What's the difference between Mm-m and Ahhh?
About 3 inches.

Why don't women like having sex with an SAS man?
They slip in and out unnoticed.

Why do married women have so many wrinkles?
It's from squinting up their eyes and saying, "Pull what?"

Said the art critic to the flasher: "Well hung, good show, Sir."

Girls, the best way to drive your fella mad is to smile in your sleep.

"Hello, I'm a little stiff from rugby."
"No problem, it doesn't matter where you come from," she replied.

"Hey, Loser!" shouted the gang of boys. "What's the difference between your sister and a Rolls-Royce?"
"None of us have been in a Rolls-Royce."

Did you hear about the man who had over 150 dogs in his house?
The doctor told him to stop whistling in his sleep.

★   ★   ★

What's the difference between condoms and coffins?
They both contain something stiff, but one's coming while the other's going.

One of the greatest mysteries that men cannot solve is why, when they get drunk, someone creeps into their bedroom in the middle of the night, vomits all down their clothes and pees in the wardrobe.

How can a weak wally make his girlfriend laugh?
By showing her his tackle.

What do men have in their underpants that women don't want on their faces?
Wrinkles.

Life is like a bed of roses...full of pricks.

What did the fat girl say to the fat boy?
Thanks for the tip.

**You can tell Samantha enjoyed herself when she was alive.
They had to bury her in a Y-shaped coffin.**

Why do estate agents' wives always get on top?
Because estate agents always fuck up.

**What do you get if you cross a rooster with a badly trained dog?
A cock that doesn't come.**

What is the difference between 365 days in a year and 365 condoms?
One's a good year and the other's a fucking good year.

A lady is a woman who doesn't drink, doesn't smoke and only curses when it slips out.

347

Words of wisdom:
The most vulnerable area for goalkeepers is between their legs.

What's the similarity between a penis and Rubik's cube?
They both get harder the longer you play with them.

It has just been announced that women no longer have to risk the dangers of breast enlargement.
Doctors have just discovered a way of making men's hands smaller.

What do you call it when an Englishman's girlfriend has an orgasm?
A miracle.

Did you hear about the wally who tried to commit rape?
He tied his victim's legs together so she couldn't run away.

Wise men say it wasn't the apple that caused all the trouble in the Garden of Eden. It was the pair on the ground!

An ageing old rook was talking to a bull in a field.

"I wish I could fly to the top of that tree, but these days, I just haven't got the energy," he said sadly.

"I've got an idea," replied the bull. "If you eat part of my droppings you'll get extra energy because they're packed with minerals and vitamins."

So the rook did as he suggested and each day ate part of the bull's droppings. Sure enough, after a couple of weeks, the rook felt so revived he soared to the top of the tree and proudly surveyed the surrounding countryside. However, he was spotted by a farmer who immediately got hold of his shotgun and killed the bird stone-dead.

"Oh dear," sighed the bull. "I should have warned him. Bull shit may get you to the top, but it doesn't mean you'll stay there."

"Hi, do you know the difference between a cocksucker and a ham sandwich?"

"No."

"Great. How about coming over for lunch tomorrow?"

349

There are three words to make a man hit rock bottom.
"Is it in?"

Did you hear about the man who so hated his mother-in-law that he cut the tail off the dog so there would be no visible signs of welcome!

A man went for a meal in a kosher restaurant and said to the waiter, "Excuse me, do you have matzoballs?"
"No sir," he replied. "It's just the way I walk."

What do good time girls have written on their underwear?
"Next."

THE GRASS IS ALWAYS GREENER

Three men were sitting on a bench high on a cliff overlooking the sea when one of them spotted an old bottle hidden in some undergrowth. He pulled it out, undid the cork and a genie appeared.

"I will grant each of you one wish," he said. "You will fling yourself off the cliff calling out whatever you would like and you will land in a boat full of that wish."

So the first man jumped off and shouted "Money" and sure enough he landed in a boat full of £50 notes.

The second man jumped off and shouted "Beautiful girls" and sure enough he landed in a boat of beautiful girls.

Then it was the turn of the third man who was a bit simple and had forgotten what he was supposed to do. He took a flying leap off the cliff and as he went down he shouted "Whee!"

A Scotsman was walking on the mountainside when he spotted a bottle hidden in the heather. It had a cork in the top and as he pulled it out a genie appeared.

"Oh thank you, thank you," said the genie. "I'm free at last and I will grant you three wishes."

351

"Well, er..." pondered the Scotsman. "I'd like the biggest bottle of whisky you can give me."

Whoosh, a 5 litre bottle of the finest whisky appeared before him and he spent the next couple of hours gulping it down. Amazingly, when it was empty it automatically filled itself up again.

"I can't believe my eyes," gasped the Scotsman.

"Well, you're seeing right," said the genie, "every time you empty the bottle it will automatically fill up. Now what would you like for your other 2 wishes?"

"Oh that's easy, I'll have another two of the same, please!"

Have you ever wondered why men like to go fishing?

It's the only time they'll hear someone say to them, "Goodness, that is a big one."

A man walked into the chemist's shop and demanded his money back.

"The ointment you sold me to make my willy bigger doesn't work," he complained angrily. "I did exactly as the instructions said which was to rub it in."

"Oh I see your problem," replied the chemist. "You didn't read the small print which says it has to be rubbed in by a woman between the ages of 18–30."

A man found an old lamp on the sea shore and as he picked it up, a genie appeared.

"You have one wish," said the genie. "What would you like?"

After thinking for a moment he replied, "I've always been a bit lacking in the nether regions, do you think I could have a bigger willy?"

"Your wish is granted."

The man walked on and as the minutes went by he realised his willy was getting longer and longer – down to the knees, down to the ankles…

The man chased back up the beach to find the genie.

"Excuse me," he said, "could have another wish?"

"What's that?" replied the genie.

"Do you think you could give me longer legs?"

"Bob came home looking utterly wretched and buried his head in his hands.

"I've been sacked," he told his wife.

"After 35 years of doing the same job, day in, day out, I have been replaced by an electronic gadget the size of a torch. And the awful thing is," he continued, "I can't fault it. It can do everything I can do, and do it better, and it will never wear out!"

Bob looked up for comfort but his wife had gone. She was down the shops looking to buy one.

353

A man walks into a chemist and says to the pharmacist, "I'm entertaining 4 girls tonight so I need something to keep me going – I don't want to go soft on them."

"I have just the thing here," replies the pharmacist and he gives the man a small bottle of pills marked "super strength". The next day the man returns to the chemist shop, drops his trousers to reveal a nasty looking shrivelled willy, all black and blue and very sore.

"Can I have a tube of muscle rub?" he asks.

"What! To put on that?" asks the pharmacist.

"Oh no, it's for my arms, the girl's didn't show up."

★ ★ ★

A man walks into a bar with a cat and an ostrich and orders three pints of beer.

"That'll be £4.60," says the barman and the man hands over the money. Sometime later, another round is ordered and when it comes to paying, the cat says "You get these ostrich, I think it's your shout."

The three stay in the bar drinking all night but no matter how many rounds they have, the cat manages to get out of paying. As the bell for last orders rings, the barman says to the man, "How come you're drinking with a cat and an ostrich?"

"Well," says the man sadly, "not long ago, I was out walking on the beach when I found an old bottle. I took out the cork and a genie appeared who said he'd grant me one wish. So I asked for a bird with long legs and a tight pussy!"

The timid, ineffectual man walked up to the beautiful young woman and said, "Excuse me, miss, would you mind accusing me of sexual harassment in front of my fellow workers?"

A middle-aged man, going grey at the temples, dyes his hair and is so pleased with the results that he has to test his new-found youth on the general public. He sets off for town passing a long queue of people at the bus stop. Going up to the first in the queue, he asks the woman if she would mind guessing his age.

She looks at him and replies, "Oh, I would say about 35."

"No, no," he answers, looking very pleased. "I'm actually 44."

He carries on to the supermarket and when he's done his shopping, he asks the girl on the till to guess his age.

"About 38," she says.

Away goes the man, very satisfied at the results and so pre-occupied with his vanity that he bumps right into an old spinster.

"I'm so sorry, miss, I didn't see you."

"That's alright, young man," she replies.

"Young man! I do indeed feel young. Would you like to guess how old I am?" he boasts.

"I'll have to feel your willy to tell you that," she says.

"Really!" he gasps. "Well okay."

So the spinster puts her hand down his trousers, feels around and says, "You're 44."

"Why! that's absolutely amazing," he says, "how can you tell?"

"I was in the bus queue earlier, when you went past."

A very vain man, who spent more time in the gym lifting weights than he did at work, decided he wanted a full-length mirror in the bathroom so he could admire himself. He went down to the local second-hand shop to see what was on offer.

"We've got plenty of mirrors, Sir," said the shopkeeper, "but if I was you, I wouldn't pick this one because it has strange powers that don't always do you any good." But the man's curiosity was aroused and he insisted on buying that particular mirror. The next morning he looked at himself in the new mirror and realised he was not as well endowed as he thought he was.

"Okay mirror," he said, "if you've really got special powers, give me a dick that touches the floor." And the man's legs fell off.

All the members of the Battersby social club went by coach to Morecambe for a day's outing where they ate a lot, played the bingo, drank a lot, paddled in the sea, drank some more, went on the funfair and drank even more.

At the end of the evening, tired but happy, they got back on the bus for home. However, half-way there, the men were feeling the effects of the beer and they all needed the toilet badly.

"I'll have to stop in the lay-by," shouted the bus driver and having done so, all the men scrambled off and peed wherever they could, not bothered about who was watching them.

The next morning at breakfast, Julie turned to Jack and said, "You men have such disgusting habits. Mind you, ours was the best" and she smiled contentedly.

Two old ex-service men were boasting about their past conquests.

"When I was in the army, I had hundreds of girls, wherever I was stationed. We soldiers were real men."

"Rubbish," replied the Admiral. "I bet I slept with far more women than you. Girls like sailors."

"Okay, okay, when did you last sleep with a woman?" demanded the soldier.

"About 1958," replied the Admiral.

"You see! You call that being a ladies' man?", said the soldier.

The Admiral looked at his watch and said scornfully, "Well, it's only 22.10 now."

LATE IN THE DAY

Johnny looks at death in a philosophical way. He first came to realise his own mortality after having a serious tonsils operation in hospital. A nurse had given him a bed bath and he found himself going stiff. Johnny had to face up to it – death ran in the family. His great, great grandfather was hanged (in Exeter Gaol) for sheep stealing where his famous last words were "can you put the rope round my waist, I've got a boil on my neck?" His great grandfather was a famous pianist who worked on the Titanic and went down very well. His own grandfather had an untimely death when he drank a bottle of wood varnish by mistake – a horrible end but a lovely finish!

AGE CATCHES UP

A little boy and his grandpa were sitting in the garden when the little boy said, "Grandpa, grandpa, see that little worm over there. I bet I can put him back into his hole."

Grandpa accepted the bet and they agreed on £5.

"You'll never be able to do it, lad, the worm is too limp to be pushed back."

The little boy disappeared inside and came back with a can of hairspray. He sprayed it all over the worm until it became as stiff as a board and then quite easily stuck it back in the hole.

"See, Grandpa, I win my bet."

Grandpa handed over £5 and said, "I'm just popping into the house, I'll be with you in a little while."

Sure enough, 10 minutes later he reappeared and handed the boy another £5.

"But Grandpa, you've already paid me," said the boy.

"Ah yes," smiled Grandpa, "but this is from your Grandma."

What's the difference between a stick-up and a hold-up?
Age.

When do you realise you're getting old?
When you have dry dreams and wet farts.

A young journalist was asked to go and interview a celebrated old colonel who had moved into the area. Now the old colonel's reputation for bravery was well documented and the journalist decided to try and get a different angle on the interview. After chatting for about 20 minutes he then asked the colonel if there had been any time when he was really frightened.

The colonel thought for a moment and then replied, "There was a time when we were deep in the jungle, on the track of a bunch of renegades, when suddenly a lion jumped out at me and roared 'Aaarrgh'. Bloody hell, I shit myself."

The journalist was thrilled with the story.

"When was that?" he asked. "When did that happen?"

"Just now when I went 'Aaarrgh,' " replied the colonel.

The social worker was doing the rounds at the local residential home and she stopped to talk to Bob who was 92. After she'd helped him to cut up his food, she noticed a bowl of nuts on a small table next to him.

"I was given them as a present," he said, "but I don't want them, You're very welcome to have them."

Now the social worker was very fond of nuts so she nibbled

362

away on them as she continued to chat to old Bob. As she was about to go she commented, "Thanks for the nuts, it's an odd present to give to someone with no teeth."

"Oh no," he replied. "When I was given them, they had chocolate on."

An old man decides he would like to join a nudist colony so he goes along to spend a day there, before joining up. He strips off, spends half an hour walking around and then, feeling tired, sits down to rest on a park bench. Moments later a beautiful young woman comes along and in no time at all he finds himself with a raging erection. On seeing this, she gets down on her knees and gives him a blow job. "This is wonderful," he thinks to himself and immediately goes along to the office to sign up. The rest of the day passes pleasantly and just before he goes home, he drops his cigarette. When he bends down to pick it up, a young man comes up behind him and does the business.

Immediately the poor old man returns to the office to cancel his subscription.

"I'm so sorry you've changed your mind," says the owner, "you seemed to like it so much."

"That's true," says the old man, "but at my age I only get excited once a month, and I'm always dropping my cigarette."

Two old ladies were on holiday in Greece and had landed up at one of the local museums. As they wandered around they came across a magnificent 12 foot statue of a greek god, naked apart from a fig leaf. One of the old ladies stood transfixed.

"Come on, Mabel," said the other. "What are you waiting for, Christmas?"

"No, just autumn," she replied.

An old man hobbled up to the ice cream counter and asked for a chocolate cornet.

"Crushed nuts?" asked the salesgirl.

"No, arthritis," he replied.

What's blue and fucks grannies?
Hypothermia.

Did you hear about the old man who went to bed and reached across for his wife's hand?

She replied, "Not tonight, Bill, I'm too tired."

What are the signs of growing older?
At the beginning it's tri weekly, then 20 years later it's try weekly, but after 65 it's try weakly!

A very old man went to the doctors to find out if he was in good working order to enjoy an active sex life.
"OK, I'll have to examine you then," said the doctor. "Drop your trousers."
"No need for that," replied the man, sticking out his index finger and his tongue.

What does an 80-year-old woman have between her knees that a 20-year-old doesn't?
Her nipples.

It was the day of the over 60s social club outing to Scarborough. After half an hour on the coach, Bert had to get up to go to the toilet. On the way back to his seat, the bus lurched and he was thrown onto the lap of an old woman, accidentally putting his hand on her huge breast as he tried to save himself.
"I'm so very sorry," he stammered, "but if your heart is as big as your breast, I'll see you in heaven."

She replied, "Oh no, dear, if your willy's as hard as I think it is, I'll see you in Scarborough."

"It's no good, Doris," said her husband. "I know we've been married for 40 years, but I'm going to move in with Alice next door."

"But why, Alf? Haven't I always been a good wife, kept you happy?"

"Yes…but Alice gives me oral sex."

"But I give you oral sex as well!" exclaimed Doris.

"I know, but you don't have Parkinson's Disease."

An old married couple stopped at a roadside cafe to have a cup of tea before resuming their journey. Thirty minutes later, the man realised he'd left his glasses on the cafe table, so they had to turn round and drive back, the woman complaining all the way about his forgetfulness. They arrived back at the cafe and as he got out of the car she said, "While you're in there, you might as well get my umbrella as well."

Did you hear about the dirty old yachtsman?
He took a young girl out to sea and asked her to toss him off.
The lifeboat is still searching for the body.

Two old ladies are waiting at the bus stop when it begins to rain.

The first woman, Pam, is smoking, so she takes a condom out of her bag, snips the end off and puts it over her cigarette to stop it getting wet.

"That's a great idea," enthuses Mabel. "I must do the same, where do you get them from?"

"Just pop into the chemist's," Pam replies.

So when they arrive in town, Mabel heads for the chemist shop and asks for a packet of condoms.

"What size would that be, Madam?" enquires the assistant.

"I'm not sure," she replies, "One that fits over a camel, please."

Two old men were sitting on a park bench commenting on life when one turned to the other and said, "Now here's an interesting thing, when I was in my 20s and got a stiffie, I couldn't bend it at all. Then in my 30s, I could bend it an inch, in my 40s, I could bend it 2 inches, then 3 inches in my 50s and now I'm going to be 60 next week. Doesn't it make you wonder how much stronger I'm going to get!"

"Let me tell you," said the drunk old man, slurring into his pint of beer, "alchohol's a dreadful thing, it killed my

wife, you know."
"I'm so sorry," replied his listener, "alcoholic was she?"
"No, no, I came home pissed and shot her."

A short-sighted spinster was ill in bed and got a visit from what she thought was the vicar. After he had been with her for some time, he left as her friend arrived.
"That was nice of the vicar to call, wasn't it?" said the spinster.
"No, dear, that was the doctor."
"Oh really," she replied, disappointed, "I thought he was very familiar."

Two little old spinsters visit the zoo for the day and end up watching the elephants. One of the spinsters finds herself close to the fence and there, not more than a few inches away, are the elephant's testicles. Unable to stop herself, she reaches out and squeezes them. All of a sudden, the elephant roars loudly, stampedes through the fence and disappears into the park.
The zoo keeper rushes up to the old spinsters and asks them what happened. When they've finished their explanation, he drops his trousers and says, "Here, you'd better squeeze mine in the same way, I've got to catch that bugger."

A rich but sleazy old man picks up a young girl in the local pub. He buys her drinks all night and then suggests they go somewhere for a late supper. To his astonishment, she agrees and suggests they go to one of the classiest clubs in town, where she orders all the most expensive food and eats the lot with gusto.

"Goodness me, do you always eat so much?" he asks.

"Only when someone wants to get into my pants!" she replies.

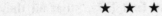

An old couple are sitting in deck chairs enjoying a few rays of sun when all of a sudden, a seagull flies overhead and drops his load on top of the man's head.

"Just a moment, dear," says the wife, "I think I've got some tissue paper in my bag."

"Don't be daft, dear, it'll be miles from here by now," he replies.

Three men were moaning about the problems that old age brings.

"Look at me," said the 70-year-old. "Every morning I'm woken by a strong urge to have a pee but when I get up and go to the bathroom I have to stand there ages before anything happens."

"I wish I had your problems," said the 80-year-old. "Every morning I go for a shit but I'm so constipated I end up being there for over 2 hours."

"Well, you're both bloody lucky," said the 90-year-old.

"Every morning at 7 o'clock, I have a good piss and shit like an elephant. The problem is…I don't wake up until 8.30."

Two women were in the kitchen listening to their husbands' conversation.

"It's incredible," said the first lady, "that all they can talk about is golf and sex."

"Oh I don't know," replied her friend. "You must remember at their ages that's all they can do – talk about it."

Two friends meet up at the over-60s social club.

"I haven't seen you in here for a few weeks," comments the first man.

"No, I've been in jail."

"In jail! What did you do?"

"Nothing. It just so happened that I was walking in the park when a beautiful young girl and a policeman rushed up and the girl accused me of sexual assault. Well, at my age, I was so flattered, I didn't deny it."

Two old men reminisce about old times.
"Do you know, Sid, when I was just a lad I never made love to my wife before we got married. Did you?"
"I can't remember," said Alf. "What was her maiden name?"

A very old woman is walking down the lane when she sees a frog waving to her.
"Oh miss," he calls. "Please help me. If you give me a kiss I will turn into a handsome film star and I promise to stay with you forever."
The old woman picks up the frog and puts it straight into her handbag.
"Hey!" shouts the frog, "Aren't you going to kiss me?"
"Oh no," she replies. "When you get to my age, what good is a handsome man? A talking frog is much more exciting."

An old woman who'd been living on her own for many years was burgled one night. They tied her up, ransacked the house and were just about to leave when the boss turned to his accomplices and said, "Wait outside, I reckon I'll just give her something to remember me by."
"Oh, come on, boss," whined the others. "Let's just get out of here before there's any trouble."

Hearing this, the old woman interrupted.
"Now hold on, don't you think you ought to leave it to the boss to decide what to do?"

Two old ladies talking over half a mild in the local pub.
"Did you hear old Sid had a massive stroke?" said one.
"Oh yes," said the other. "Everyone knew, that's why he was so popular with the ladies."

"Look, Flo," said the old spinster, "they're selling 3 cucumbers for 60p."
"Well, I can always eat the other two," came the reply.

He was so old that when he asked the doctor how long he might live, the doctor replied, "I wouldn't advise you to buy any green bananas."

A man who lived at a nudist colony received a letter from his mother asking him to send her a more up-to-date photo of himself. Unfortunately, he only had one picture, but it was of him in the nude, so he cut the photo in half and sent her the top half. Some time later, mum wrote again asking him if he would send a photo of himself to his ageing grandmother. Now he only had the bottom half left but because she had such poor eyesight, he took a chance that she would be none the wiser. Some time later, he got a letter back from his grandmother and in it she said, "Thanks for the picture. Maybe you should change your hairstyle a bit, though, it makes your nose look long."

Two old seadogs were mulling over old times in the Black Dog Public House. One had a wooden leg and the other had an eye patch and a hook on the end of his arm.

"So how did you lose your leg?" asked one-eyed Jack.

"It were back in '49. Our ship went down in rough seas off the coast of China and some bloody big shark came along and bit it off. The bastard! So what about you and your hook?"

"That was down to Hardacre's lads. They chased us halfway across the channel before boarding us. But we put up a great fight. Shook the beggars off in the end. Just a shame it wasn't before one of them cut my arm off."

"And what about the eye patch?"

"Seagull shit."

"What! I don't believe it."

"As true as I'm sitting here," said Jack. "I happened to look up at the sun and this seagull shat in my eye."

"And that's what made you blind?"

"No, but it was only the second day with my new hook."

Two old women lived in the most boring old people's home ever.

There was nothing to do but watch TV, play bingo or knit.

"Let's liven this place up a bit," said one to the other. "Why don't we give the men a thrill and streak past them as they're all sitting in their deckchairs.

The other agreed and later in the day, they carried out their plan.

"Did you see that?" one old man asked his companion.

"I did," he replied "but my eyes aren't so good these days, who were they and what were they wearing?"

"I don't know who they were, but whatever they were wearing, it needed ironing."

Sweet old Fay Mahoney hobbled along to confession as she'd done for more than 70 years. She went in, sat down and began. "Forgive me Father for I have sinned. I committed adultery with a young, good-looking milkman."

"Oh my goodness," said the shocked priest, "and when was this?"

"About fifty years ago, but I just felt like remembering the good old days."

DEAD ENDS

A man was lying on his death bed, time was running out and his family were standing round about.

"Joe, Joe," whispered his wife, "is there anything I can do for you? Do you have a last wish?"

Joe lifted his head slowly from the pillow and sniffed the air. He could smell his wife's baking in the oven.

"Can I have just a last slice of the wonderful cake you're baking?" he croaked.

"I'm afraid not, Joe, that's for the funeral."

The two men had just reached the 10th hole when a funeral procession went slowly by. The first man stopped playing, took his hat off and bowed his head.

"That was very good of you," said the second man.

"Well, it's only right. We were married 27 years and she was a good wife to me," he replied.

"You knew we were going out tonight, yet you spent even longer on the golf course today," she yelled.

"I'm sorry, love, it couldn't be helped," replied her husband.

"Old Cyril dropped dead on the 11th hole so from then on

in we played a hole, dragged Cyril, played a hole, dragged Cyril..."

On the death of her husband, Eva placed a notice in the local newspaper.
"Robert Percy, aged 62, died of VD on June 7, at 3pm."
The next day, she met her friend in the street and her friend asked her, somewhat puzzled, "But Eva, I thought you told me he died of a bowel complaint?"
"He did," she replied, "but I'd prefer people to remember him as a great lover rather than the little shit he really was."

"Oh doctor," said the man as he regained consciousness, "tell me please, was the operation successful?"
"I'm sorry," came the reply, "I'm not the doctor, I'm an angel."

★ ★ ★

It was the funeral of John's wife and he sat crying his eyes out in the front pew. He seemed inconsolable, so the Vicar decided to go over and have a word.
"I'm so sorry, John, I know this is a difficult time for you but the pain will eventually lessen. You're still quite a young man and maybe you'll meet someone else one day."
John stopped sobbing and looked up at the Vicar.

"It's alright for you to say that, Vicar," he complained, "but where am I going to get a fuck tonight?"

Three nuns arrived at the Pearly Gates and each was asked a question before they were allowed to enter. The first nun was asked to name the first man.
"Adam," she replied, and the gates opened for her.
The second nun was asked to name the first woman.
"Eve," she replied, and again the gates opened.
Then a question was put to the third nun.
"What were the first words that Eve said to Adam?"
"Gosh! That is a hard one," she replied, and once more the gates opened for her to go inside.

The finest batsman the county had ever had was killed in a bad car crash and one of the substitute cricketers thought it was time he showed what he could do.
"Listen, boss, how about me taking his place?" he asked.
"Well, I'm not sure," replied the manager. "We'll have to see what the undertakers say first."

One of Ireland's greatest footballers died and went to heaven where he was met by an angel at the Pearly Gates.

"Is there any reason why you think you should not be allowed in?" asked the angel.

The footballer thought for a moment and then replied, "Actually there was an international match that I played in, Ireland against England, and I purposefully fell over in the box so that we were awarded a penalty. It helped us to beat England 2–1."

"Well, it's not the most serious mistake I've ever heard so you may come in."

"Oh that's wonderful, I've always regretted that moment... thank you so much, St Peter."

"Think nothing of it," said the angel.

"Oh, by the way, I'm not St Peter, it's his day off, I'm St Patrick."

An old couple, married for over 50 years, die within a week of each other and arrive in heaven at the same time.

Once the paperwork has been seen to, an angel escorts them to their new accommodation. After living in a small terraced cottage all their lives, the new house is like a palace. Set in two acres of land, it has its own swimming pool and a double garage with "his" and "hers" cars. The old man turns to his wife in astonishment and says, "Well, bugger me, Pam, if you hadn't stopped us drinking and smoking, we'd have been enjoying all this years ago."

On the day of Jack's funeral, the undertakers took his coffin up to the church in a coach and four black horses. Now the church was at the top of a steep hill and suddenly, without warning, the doors of the coach flew open and the coffin careered back down the hill. By the time it reached the bottom, it was going a fair pace and smashed through the doors of the chemist shop, hitting the counter and bursting open.

"Aaargh," screamed the assistant as Jack sat up and said, "Can you give me something to stop me coughing?"

Dawn's husband had just been cremated, the mourners had gone home and she was left holding his ashes. She said to the ashes, "Well, Dave, I've got a few things to say to you. See this fancy ring on my finger, the one I always wanted and the one you would never buy me? Well, I've bought it. And you see this flashy leather handbag with matching shoes? You always promised, but never got round to it. Well, I've bought them too. She then tipped his ashes onto the ground and blew on them, saying scornfully, "So there you are, Dave, that's the blow job you always wanted and never got."

"Hello, John, how are you?" asked the barman. "How are you managing since your wife died?"

"Not too bad," replied John, "the sex is just the same, but the washing up clogs the sink."

Two men lived next door to each other for over 20 years but they couldn't have been more different. Sam was a model citizen, church every Sunday, a parish counsellor and a charity worker. Geoff was a drinker, gambler and a man for the ladies. Eventually Geoff died, he was quite young but the riotous life did him no favours. Then 15 years later, Sam passed away and arrived in heaven where he was astonished to see his ex-next-door neighbour lounging on a cloud, a huge barrel of beer next to him and a naked lady sitting on his lap.

"Why, that's outrageous!" exclaimed Sam. 'I strive to be a good citizen on earth so that I might enjoy the fruits of heaven and when I get here I see Geoff. He should have been in hell."

"Oh he's in hell alright," said the angel, "That beer barrel's got a hole in it...and the woman hasn't."

The undertakers were having a very difficult time. They couldn't get the coffin lid down on old Arthur because he'd died with a full erection. Eventually, they had to ring his wife and on hearing the problem, she told them to cut it off and stick it up his backside.

On the day of the funeral, Arthur's wife took one more look at her dead husband before he was taken away and she noticed a pained expression on his face. She whispered, "That'll teach you, you old sod, you should have believed me when I said it hurt."

"Ladies and gentlemen, we are here today to bid farewell to our departed neighbour, old Bob Flowers. Is there anyone in the congregation who would like to say a few nice words about him?" asked the vicar.
But there was silence.
"Come on now, don't be shy, someone must remember something good about him."
Still no response.
"Please, someone say something," pleaded the harassed vicar. All of a sudden, a voice was heard at the back of the church.
"His brother was worse."

Flo is devastated when her husband dies so her friends eventually persuade her to see a spiritualist so that she can get in touch with him again. All goes according to plan and her late husband is contacted.
"Are you alright, Martin? What do you get up to all day?"
"Hello, Flo. Yes, I'm okay. Well I wake up in the morning, go

for a swim, have something to eat, make love to some of the girls, have another swim, eat more food and then have a snooze."

"My goodness," says Flo, "you've changed a bit, you never did those sort of things down here."

"No, but I wasn't a duck then."

A very successful businessman was lying on his death bed. Just before the end he whispered, "Cheryl, are you there?"

"Yes, Jack, I'm here."

"Tom, are you there?"

"Yes, dad, I'm here."

"Richard, are you there?"

"Yes, dad," he sobbed. "I'm here."

Suddenly Jack jerked himself up and shouted angrily, "So who's minding the fucking business then?"

An old woman had been going to the same doctor for over 50 years and during that time had made his life a living hell by constantly complaining about one thing after another.

Eventually, however, she died and was buried in the local churchyard, but it was less than a month later that the doctor also died and was buried in the next plot to her. For a few minutes after the mourners had gone all was quiet and then the doctor heard tapping on the side of his coffin.

"What is it now, Mrs Mowner?" he sighed.
"Can you give me something for worms, doctor?"

It was the funeral of Big John Nowall, the most arrogant man
in the district. As his coffin passed into the church, one of
the spectators turned to the other and said, "I can't believe
Big John's in there, the coffin looks so small."
"Oh that's easy to explain," came the reply, "once they let all
the bullshit out of him, he fitted perfectly."

Asked to identify her missing husband, Beryl went along to
the morgue but on pulling back the sheet she shook her
head sadly. "No, that's not him," she said, looking at the
man's sizeable parts, "but some poor woman's lost a good
friend."

Two Scotsmen are talking in the pub and one turns to the
other, saying, "Now, Mick, if I should die first, will you pour
a bottle of the finest malt whisky over my grave?"
"That I will," says Jock, "but do you mind if it goes through
my kidneys first?"

One evening, there was a knock on the O'Flannagans' door. "Hello Mary," said Sean. "I've got some bad news for you. There's been a terrible accident down at the brewery and Pat is dead."

"Oh no, my poor husband!" sobbed Mary as she collapsed on the ground. "What happened?"

"It wasn't a pretty sight," sighed Sean. "Pat fell into a huge vat of Guinness and I'm afraid he drowned."

"Aaagh!" wept Mary and for some minutes nothing more was said. Eventually, Mary roused herself and said to Sean. "I hope it was all over quickly?"

"I'm afraid not. He came out four times to take a pee."

★ ★ ★